# GUIDE TO READING THE CHINESE ALMANAC

# GUIDE TO READING THE CHINESE ALMANAC

By Dr Stephen Skinner

with Man-Ho Kwok, Wei Loon Soo and Hsiao-Hung Pai

Edited by Bruce Laird
Design by Stuart Jones

GOLDEN HOARD PRESS
2019

Published by Golden Hoard Press Pte Ltd
PO Box 1073
Robinson Road PO
Singapore 902123
www.GoldenHoard.com


First Edition

Reproduced with permission from *Feng Shui for Modern Living* magazine Vol. 1, Nos 1-30
www.FengShui.net


© 2019 Stephen Skinner
www.SSkinner.com


All rights reserved. No part of this publication may be reproduced or utilized in any form or by any means, electronic or mechanical, including printing, photocopying, uploading to the web, recording, or by any information storage and retrieval system, or used in another book, without specific written permission from the authors, except for short fully credited extracts or quotes used for review purposes.


ISBN: 978-1-912212262


Printed by Kindle

# Contents

|   | | |
|---|---|---|
|   | Introduction | 7 |
| 1 | Deciphering the Chinese Almanac | 14 |
| 2 | The feng shui Directions and Spirits | 16 |
| 3 | Interpreting the Stars of the Year | 18 |
| 4 | The Sexagenary Cycle and Birth dates | 20 |
| 5 | The feng shui effect of the 24 seasons | 22 |
| 6 | Magical Talismans in the Almanac | 24 |
| 7 | The 28 Constellations & four Palaces | 26 |
| 8 | Lunar Month of your birthday | 28 |
| 9 | Lighting the Lamps: the Planets | 30 |
| 10 | Coin divination for the *Yijing* | 32 |
| 11 | Eclipses and the four Celestial animals | 34 |
| 12 | Face and hand reading in the Almanac | 36 |
| 13 | Festivals & reading the daily portents | 38 |
| 14 | The Heart of the Almanac | 40 |
| 15 | Reading the Daily columns | 42 |
| 16 | The Years and the body of the Emperor | 44 |
| 17 | Pregnancy, choosing a good Partner | 46 |
| 18 | Yarrow stalks, palm reading, omens | 48 |
| 19 | Graves, generating prosperity with yin feng shui | 50 |
| 20 | Identification of features on a feng shui map | 52 |
| 21 | The 8 Directions of Good & Bad Stars on the New Year map | 54 |
| 22 | The 28 Chinese Constellations | 56 |
| 23 | The 24 Stars like Tian-fu, Tzu-wei and Wen-chang | 58 |
| 24 | Balancing the White Tiger | 60 |
| 25 | Animal Sign compatibilities | 62 |
| 26 | The Twelve Palaces | 64 |
| 27 | Twelve life stages | 66 |
| 28 | Analysis of every column of the monthly calendar tables | 68 |

# Introduction

This book is about the Chinese Almanac or *Tung Shu* 通書, whose story stretches back into the distant past of Chinese history. Amazingly it sells as many as three million copies a year, in its various forms in Hong Kong, Taiwan, Macau, Singapore, Malaysia, Thailand, Philippines, Indonesia and other areas with Chinese populations. The first *Tung Shu* translated into English was published by Master Victor Dy in Manila in the late 20th century. Later, versions appeared produced by GM Raymond Lo in Hong Kong, Joey Yap in Malaysia, and GM Tan in Singapore.

Originally called the *Tung Shing*, it began as a Calendar which legend attributes to Huangdi, the semi-mythical Yellow Emperor (reputed to have reigned 2698–2598 BCE) who was seen as the founder of much of Chinese culture. The traditional first date of publication is 2256 BCE. This event of first publication is mentioned in the *Shujing: the Canon of Yao* (Part 1, Book 2), which explains that the Emperor Yao commanded two officials to correlate the lunar and solar dates in order to benefit the ordinary people, thereby bringing the ritual lunar calendar into line with the solar astronomical calendar. He commanded these officials to calculate and delineate the movements of the sun, the moon, the stars in relation to the Ecliptic and so to outline the seasons which could then be utilised and observed by the people. Subsequently one of the major marks of Imperial authority and power was the right and ability to produce an accurate yearly calendar. "By ordering and assisting agriculture, by giving warning of eclipses and movements in the heavens, the Emperor showed he was a true 'son of Heaven,' ruling by and with the supreme authority of Heaven."[1] To understand the cycles of time and tide was seen as also being able to control them. Apart from the Imperial significance, the agrarian content ensured this book was central to Chinese life, then as it still is now.

It is fairly certain that wood-block printed Almanacs have been around since the ninth century (see Figure 1). In 835 CE the writer Feng Su asserted that:

> In all the provinces of Szechwan and Huainan, printed calendars are on sale in the markets. Every year, before the Imperial Observatory has submitted the new calendars for approval and had it officially promulgated, these printed calendars have flooded the empire. This violates the principle that (the Calendar) is a gift of His Majesty.[2]

Even then the Emperor was struggling to maintain his monopoly on the printing of the Almanac. Note that this wood-block printing was occurring more than 600 years before Gutenberg invented printing for the Western world.

---

[1] Palmer (1986), p. 15.
[2] Quoted by Mark Elvin in *The Pattern of the Chinese Past*, Stanford University Press, 1973, p. 181.

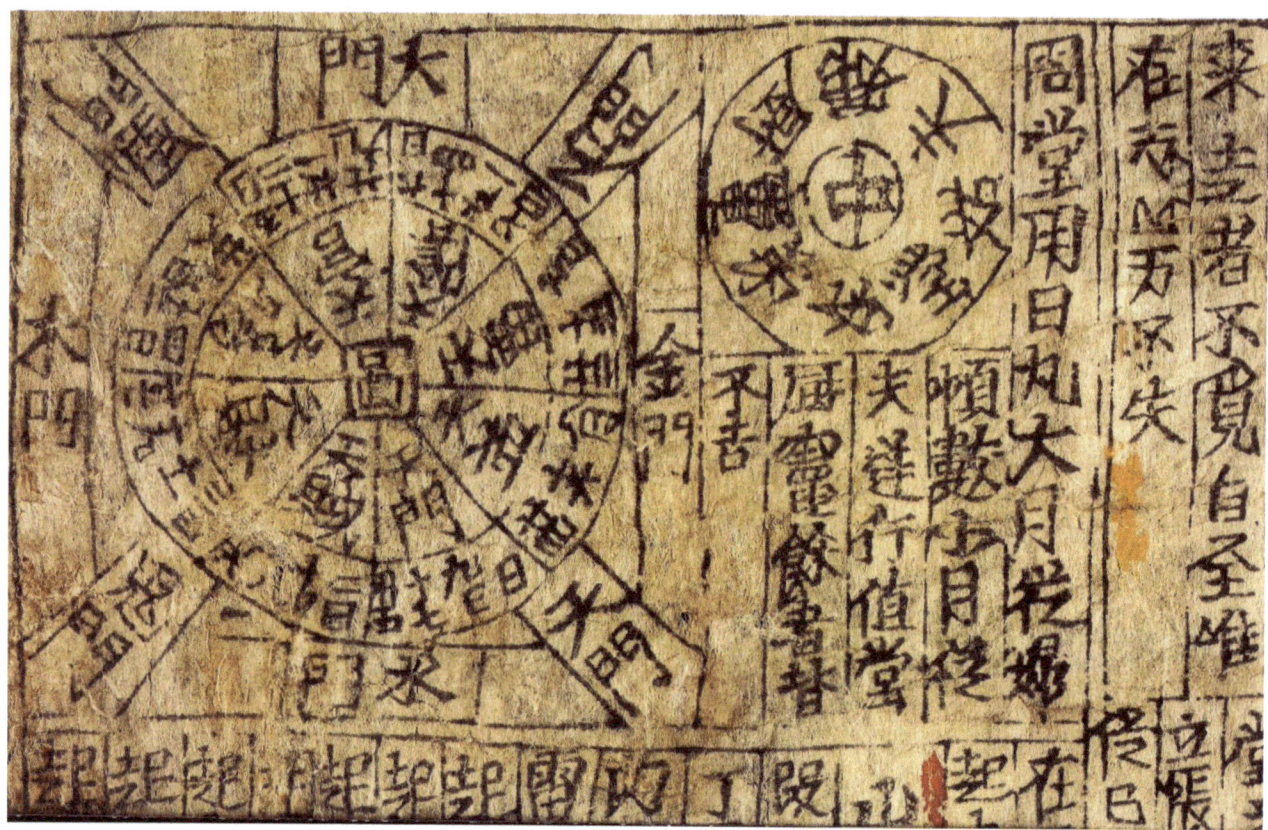

Figure 1: The Directions and Positions Diagram page from a *Tung Shu* dating from the ninth century (877 CE). Courtesy of the British Museum.

The Almanac has changed its form numerous times throughout the years over many dynasties. By the Qing dynasty it was re-named the Tung Shu (通書). Tung (通) means 'all' and Shu (書) means 'book,' so *Tung Shu* could be literally interpreted as the 'Know Everything Book,' or maybe the 'Book of the Myriad Things.' In Cantonese in Hong Kong it became known as the *Tong Sing*, meaning 'Good Luck in Everything.' The Almanac is also known as the *Farmers' Calendar*, because of its section on the 24 mini-Seasons which helps with planting and harvesting time indications.

The art of selecting auspicious days was formed and improved in the Han Dynasty (206 BC - 220 CE). Most of the writings after the Han Dynasty and prior to the Yuan Dynasty (1271 - 1368 AD) have been lost, making it difficult to trace the history. The most detailed and representative literature on picking auspicious days available today is *Xie Ji Bian Fang Shu* compiled during the reign of Emperor Qianlong (1711 - 1799 CE) of the Qing Dynasty.

During the Qing dynasty the production of the Almanac was the responsibility of the Imperial Bureau of Astronomy and Department of Calendrical Studies, but nowadays it is constructed by astrologers in Taiwan and Hong Kong. Perhaps the best known of these was Choi Pak Lai (see Figure 2) who sadly passed away in 2018. His Almanac calculations also formed the basis of a number of other abridged almanacs issued each year, including those in the Chinese edition of *Feng Shui for Modern Living*.

Figure 2: Choi Pak Lai, perhaps the most famous Hong Kong Almanac astrologer of recent years.

The core of the Almanac is a daily calendar based on the Chinese lunar calendar (combined with the solar calendar), giving advice on the best days to do certain things, such as marriage, travel, renovation, house moving or contract signings. This is supplemented by a fascinating range of subjects, with many pages devoted to divination, astrology, feng shui, fortune telling methods, predictions, physiognomy, palmistry, talismans, herbal medicine, numerology, moral codes, stories, legends, and even pregnancy diagrams showing the development of the foetus over the nine months. Older versions often had a mini Chinese-English word list and numeric telegraphic codes for Chinese words.

The current format is derived from the Qing dynasty and has a continuous publication history dating back over 200 years. See Figure 3 for an example of the Directions page from the last published Qing Almanac. After that, government calendar calculations adopted a Western calendar and sought to distance themselves from the Imperial format, at which point the traditional format was carried on instead by private publishers.

One of the most important pages for astrologers and feng shui practitioners is the 'Year Spirits[3] Direction and Positions Diagram,' which occurs in the first 3 pages of every Almanac.

---

[3] *Shen.*

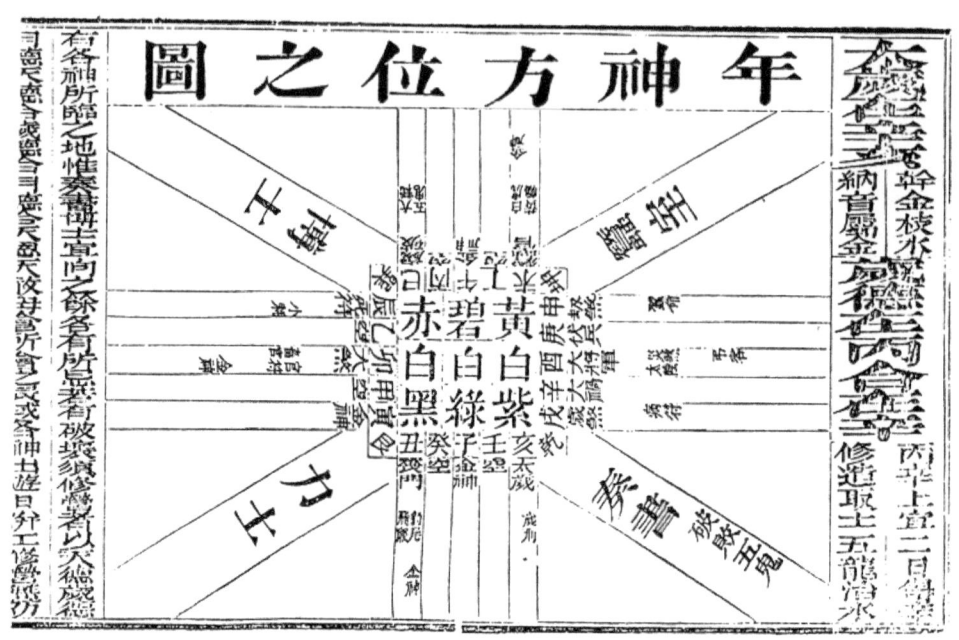

Figure 3: The 'Year Spirits Direction and Positions Diagram' page from a Qing Dynasty Almanac for 1911 (the last year of Qing rule) showing the feng shui configuration for that year.[4]

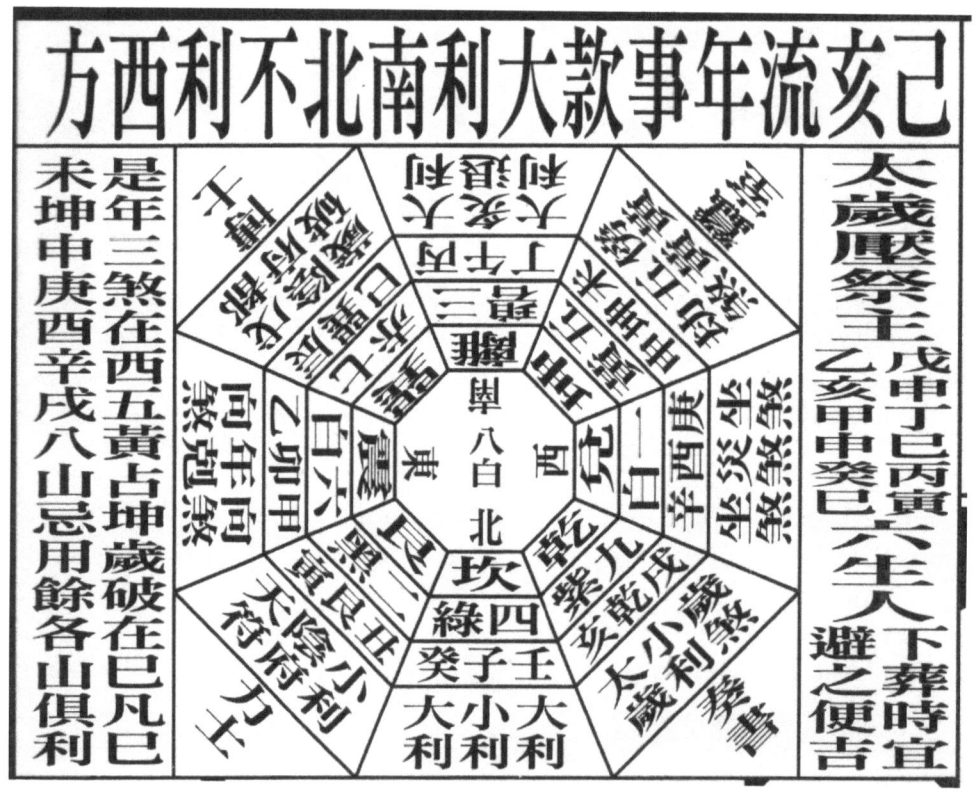

Figure 4: The 'Year Spirits Direction and Positions Diagram' page from a 2019 Almanac.

---

[4] *Shi Hsian Shu* 時憲書 *Shi Xian Shu*, 1911.

The same arrangement has persisted but with the square arrangement morphing into an octagonal form, but carrying the same information, with the Flying Stars shown in the second octagonal ring from the centre. Other astrological pages include the 28 unequal *Xiu* or Mansions of the Moon, which are here personified, each with its spirit talismanic seal and name (Figure 5). Daoist talismans purely for health or for deterring evil spirits also have their sections (Figure 6)

Figure 5: Seven of the 28 *Xiu* or Asterisms as illustrated in a modern *Tung Shu*.

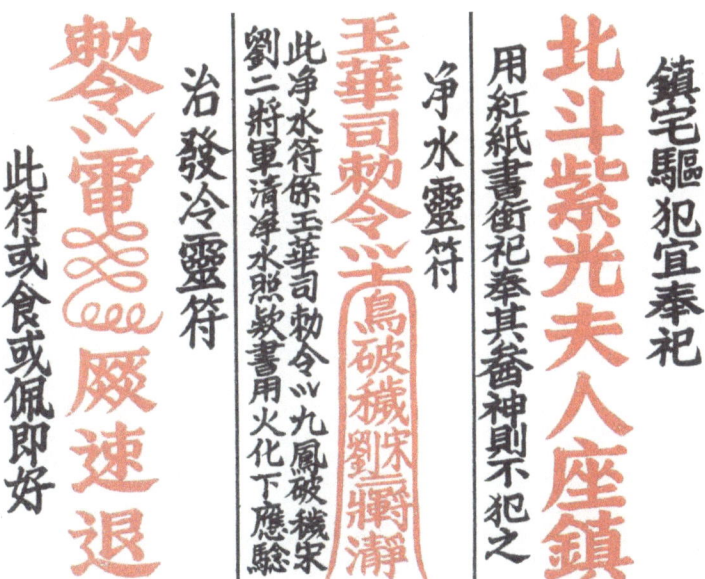

Figure 6: Daoist talismans: to protect your house from evil influences; to purify the water in a well; and to cure a fever. In each case specific instructions need to be followed to ensure its effectiveness.

*Typical contents of the Tung Shu*

Every Almanac may include one or more of the following sections:

Astrological Characteristics of the 100 most recent years
Auspicious and Inauspicious Dates for various activities
Auspicious and Inauspicious Directions and Stars of the coming Year
Auspicious and Inauspicious Directions and Stars of the current Year
Auspicious Times for Miscellaneous Activities
Biscuit Poem of Liu Po Wen
'Bone weight' astrology derived from year, month, day and time of birth
Charms designed to protect the foetus and spirits guarding the childhood years
Chinese Festival dates
Chinese Writing Styles
Coin Divination
Cup Divination of Tu Di
Current Year Calendar
Daoist talismans
Day calculations on the hand
Deity in Charge based on Year of Birth
Divination by sneezes and facial twitches
Duke of Zhou's Book of Dreams
Explanation of Eclipses - astronomy
Face Reading
Forecast for each of the 12 Animals
Fortune Telling by Physical Sensations
Ghost Catcher Zhang Tian Shih and his Talismans
Guide to Household Management
Guide to Running a Small Business
Hundred Chinese Family Names
Hundred Year Astrological Calendar Characters
Influence of the Five Elements on Childhood
Interpreting facial moles
Jia Zi Cycles (Stems and Branch combinations) showing Good and Bad Stars
Judging People by their Habits
Letter Writing and Invitation Etiquette
Lucky Direction of the Day
Master Dong's Date Selection Methods
Palmistry
Personal Fortune of the Year
Pronunciation of English Words
Receiving the God of Wealth
Secret book of Zhu Ge - fortune Telling by the Number of Strokes in a name
Song of Interpreting Personalities
Spring Festival Cow agricultural predictions for the coming year
Spring Festival Cow agricultural predictions for the current year
Sunrise and Sunset Times for the 24 Mini-Seasons

Table of Auspicious and Inauspicious Dates
Telegram Numeration of Chinese Characters
The Yellow Emperor's Poem of the Four Seasons
Timing of Daily activities
Traditional Children's Stories about Confucius
Traditional Medical Prescriptions
Twenty-eight Constellations or *Xiu*
Twenty-four Mini-Seasons (*Jie* and *Qi*)
Twenty-six Malignant Gates
Weather and Farming Forecast
Writing Auspicious Characters in 100 different ways
*Yijing* 64 Hexagram divination
Yin Yang Calendar Comparison Table – Lunar and Solar year

Although today many of the sections of the *Tung Shu* may not be comprehensible to the average reader, for those versed in Chinese astrology or feng shui this volume is a veritable goldmine. Symptomatic of the expected frequency of its use, some editions even have a chain loop or red thread inserted into the spine so they may be easily hung on an easily accessible hook or nail.

*References:*

Lo, Raymond & Georgia Kiafi. *Chinese Almanac: the book of Auspicious days 2020.* Hong Kong, 2019.

Palmer, Martin. *T'ung Shu: the Ancient Chinese Almanac.* Boston: Shambhala, 1986. ISBN 978-0-3947422-1-2.

Skinner, Stephen. *Guide to the Feng Shui Compass,* Singapore: Golden Hoard, 2008. ISBN 978-0-9547639-9-2. pp. 197-198, 312-319.

So, Peter. *Your Fate in 2020: The Year of the Rat.* Hong Kong: Forms, 2019. ISBN: 978-96214708-8-1.

Tan Khoon Yong. *2019 Way Almanac: All-Knowing Book.* Singapore: Way Fengshui, 2018. ISSN 25297937.

Yap, Joey. *Weekly Tong Shu Diary 2020.* Kuala Lumpur: JY, 2019.

# THE CHINESE ALMANAC

## 1 a brief history

# Reading

WE BEGIN THE FIRST OF A SERIES OF ARTICLES WHICH WILL DECIPHER THE MYSTERIES OF THE CHINESE ALMANAC WITH THE HELP OF MAN-HO KWOK

Central to Chinese lifestyle and feng shui is the Chinese red covered Almanac. Today most Chinese call it the *T'ung Shu* or *T'ung Shing* the latter being the preferred term because *Shing* sounds like win in Chinese, whereas *Shu* sounds like 'lost'.

The *T'ung Shu* dates back thousands of years. Historical records have revealed animal bones and shells which were marked with the same star names used in the Almanac today.

The origins of the *T'ung Shu* can be associated with Emperor Yao, a celebrated emperor who was believed to have reigned between 2357-2255 BC. Yao ordered the *Ch'in T'ien Chien* (the Board of Astronomy) to calculate the Almanac and instructed officials to distribute copies of the Almanac to every part of his Empire.

At that time the *T'ung Shu* was only allowed to be calculated and printed by the Board of Astronomy. Any citizen who flouted this law by printing and distributing their own version would be punished by decapitation or were exiled to an army post on the outskirts of the Chinese empire never to return.

The *T'ung Shu* was later renamed the *Wang Li* (The Emperor's law or Almanac) At this time it was made up of just 15 to 16 pages. Essentially, it included calculations using the 10 Heavenly Stems and the 12 Earthly Branches to measure time on the cyclical basis of 60 combinations, one combination for each year.

China at that time was a farming community, and so was dependent upon the weather for their living. Once word spread of the Almanac and its accurate predictions of the four seasons, the people began to pressure the Emperor to take away its exclusivity and to make it available to all. Under this pressure the Emperor eventually gave-in and allowed the general distribution of the *Wang Li*.

Every winter, a new *Wang Li* was written in accordance with the change of stars which in simple terms predicted the weather for the year to come.

Because of the popularity and mass use of the Almanac its name was again later changed to *Nung Min Li*, meaning the Peasants Almanac.

Nowadays, the Almanac is a lot more complex, involving various forms of divination combined with *yin* and *yang* predictions, the Four Seasons, and 12 or 13 lunar months of the year. **MAN-HO KWOK**

First you should be aware that being written in Chinese, the Almanac must be read from the opposite direction to a Western book, beginning at the 'back'.

On the first page of the Chinese Almanac for 1998 shown on the opposite page, is the traditional illustration of the Spring Festival Cow for 1998. This picture and its associated text traditionally predicts the weather, farming business and harvest prospects for the coming year. Each year the picture changes subtley.

This page also indicates the dates on which the earth god *T'u Ti* or *Tu Wang* is supposed to be active. This is helpful to farmers who want to choose the best day for planting their crops. This parallels the old European tradition of only sowing crops at particular phases of the moon.

From a feng shui point of view the days on which the earth god is active are days on which you should not cut or dig the earth, an excellent excuse perhaps for not doing the gardening! But more seriously, it is the days on which you should avoid making feng shui changes which involve excavation such as the digging of fish ponds.

Each of the 12 sections below the picture refer to each of the 12 lunar months in 1998, starting with the first month in the middle of the right hand side of the page, and finishing with the twelfth month in the bottom left hand corner.

# the Chinese Almanac

**Yin**

**Yin**, one of the 12 Earthly Branches, which indicates the year of the Tiger or 1998

**Wu**

**Wu**, one of the 10 Heavenly Stems, which taken together with *Yin* identify the year

These pages are taken from the Almanac for 1998.

# THE CHINESE ALMANAC

## 2 a brief history

**WE CONTINUE THE SERIES OF ARTICLES WHICH WILL DECIPHER THE MYSTERIES OF THE CHINESE ALMANAC WITH THE HELP OF MAN-HO KWOK**

The second page of the Almanac is a key page for feng shui practitioners, perhaps the most important page.

The top third of the page is taken up by an octogram showing the Eight Directions, with South shown at the top. Effectively, this is the feng shui compass or *lo pan* for this year 1998. Although it is drawn as an octagram, it can be read just like a circular compass. It shows general information plus attributions which are specific to this year.

The bottom half is devoted to the 24 'mountains', which is another way of expressing the 24 Directions. The Chinese character for 'mountain' is three vertical strokes, like three peaks connected at the bottom.

This page indicates which of the Eight Directions is suitable, for example, for digging ground, or for the location of your main door or for building new property or an extension.

During the Year of the Tiger (1998) there are two particularly good luck Directions and one bad luck Direction. East and West are the best Directions, whilst North is the direction to avoid. This of course only applies for 1998 and is only a very general indication which should be modified by the month or day and by reference to your own date of birth when calculating your good and bad Directions.

These summary details are expanded in other charts in the Almanac which we will examine in later in the book.

# Reading

**Inner Ring**

The Inner Ming Tang – The centre of the compass (or first 'ring') contains the four Directions, clockwise from the top, South, West, North and East, with the Centre in the middle.

**Second Ring**

The second 'ring' of this octagonal compass, working outwards, shows the Eight Directions based on the Eight Trigrams. This is fixed and is the same from year to year.

**Third Ring**

The third 'ring' gives the colours of each of these Eight Directions, plus the eight numbers.

**Outer Corners**

The four corners contain the four ancient compass bearings.

# the Chinese Almanac

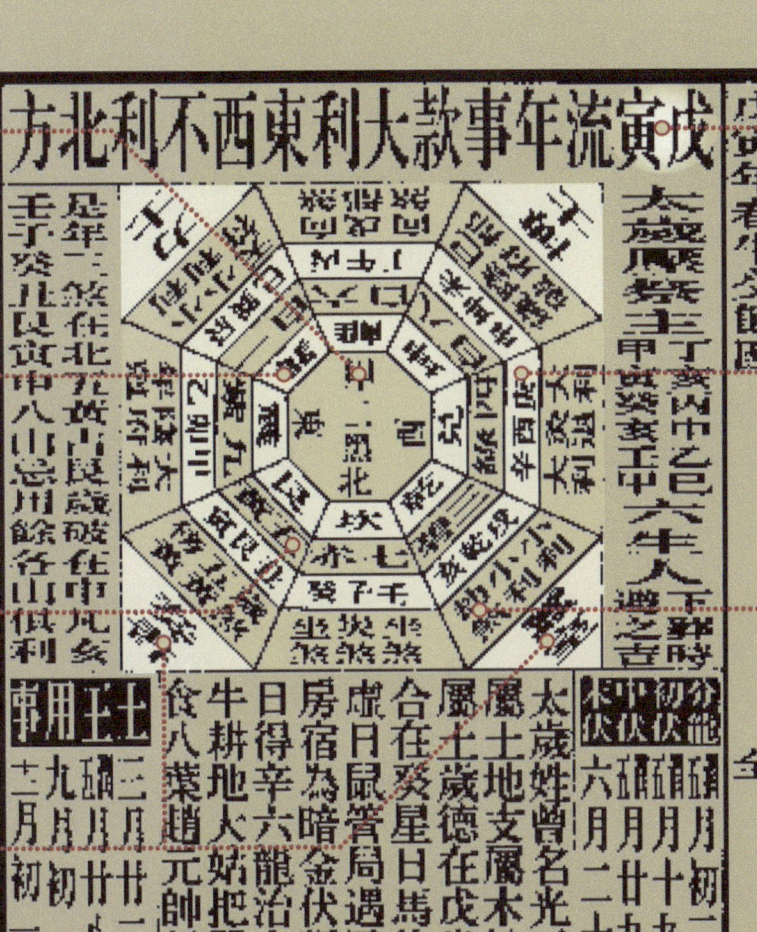

### The Heavenly Stem And The Earthly Branch

Beside and around the compass are the specific Directions for this year. In the top righthand corner the first character shows the Heavenly Stem for this year and the second character (reading right to left) shows the Earthly Branch, which for 1998 indicates the Year of the Tiger.

### Fourth Ring

The fourth 'ring' is the Stem and Branch combinations for each of the 12 'double hours' of the day and these do not change from year to year.

### Fifth Ring

The fifth 'ring' contains details of where various good and bad 'spirits' are dwelling during this year. It also shows the spirit name for the god of wealth, which changes every year, and is different for each Direction. The Chinese believe that to 'receive' the God of Wealth correctly at the beginning of the year brings Wealth throughout the year.

# THE CHINESE ALMANAC
## 3
### a brief history

# Reading

WE CONTINUE THE SERIES OF ARTICLES WHICH WILL DECIPHER THE MYSTERIES OF THE CHINESE ALMANAC WITH THE HELP OF MAN-HO KWOK

T'ung Shu, the Chinese Almanac, parts of which date back for over 4000 years, still shapes and influences the lives of millions of Chinese everyday. Translated, it literally means 'The Book of Many Things'. However, in Cantonese it is often referred to as the T'ung Sing which means 'Good Luck in Everything'. The T'ung Shu is revered and seen by many to have spiritual powers. People keep it in their homes almost as a talisman, believing that owning a copy will bring them good fortune. The Almanac is considered a book of great importance, and used as a guide in their daily lives.

The Almanac is an accumulation of information from over 3000 years, with extensive contributions from shamans, Taoists, Buddhists, Moslems, and Christians. Not only is it significant in the study of the history of religion, but it is also one of the most comprehensive and traditional sources of Chinese beliefs and practices. The T'ung Shu originated as a calendar, explaining the detail of the lunar farmer's calendar and the seasons, but now includes everything from fortune-telling to herbal medicine, including numerology, palmistry, divination, physiognomy, pregnancy charts, moral codes, dictionaries, charms, talismans, and predictions. The Almanac gives astronomical details, telegram and telex charts, plus it contains interesting stories and legends, all coming from very diverse sources. Of course it also includes a calendar of auspicious and inauspicious days, which people turn to for daily predictions to see if a specific day is lucky or not for planning important events like weddings and travel.

The Almanac was written by the most senior officials within the Chinese bureaucracy and the Imperial Court, but is now constructed annually by astrologers in Hong Kong and Taiwan.

On the fourth page of the Chinese Almanac (reading from the back) you will find a chart which indicates the influences acting on your personal fortune for this year.

- The centre block of four large characters simply indicates that this is the page concerned with your general good and bad luck for the year. It never changes.

- The 12 characters that are printed in white octagons on black or red squares are the 12 Earthly Branches. For example, this Branch, *tzu* corresponds to people born in the years 1948, 1960, 1972, 1984 and every 12 years thereafter representing the year of the Rat.

- The Lucky Stars relevant to this Branch. You can see that by the presence of only 2 Lucky Stars that anyone born under the influence of Branch *Tzu* will not generally have strong good luck that year.

- The Unlucky Stars relevant to this Branch. You can see that anyone born in a year corresponding with *tzu* fell under eight Unlucky Stars in 1998.

The 12 Earthly Branches always stay the same, whilst the lucky and unlucky star combinations fluctuate from year to year. The proportion of lucky stars to unlucky stars gives you a rough guide to the proportion of your good and bad luck for the year. Of course, this 'background' Heaven luck can be considerably modified and improved by your own efforts (Man luck) or by feng shui (Earth luck).

# the Chinese Almanac

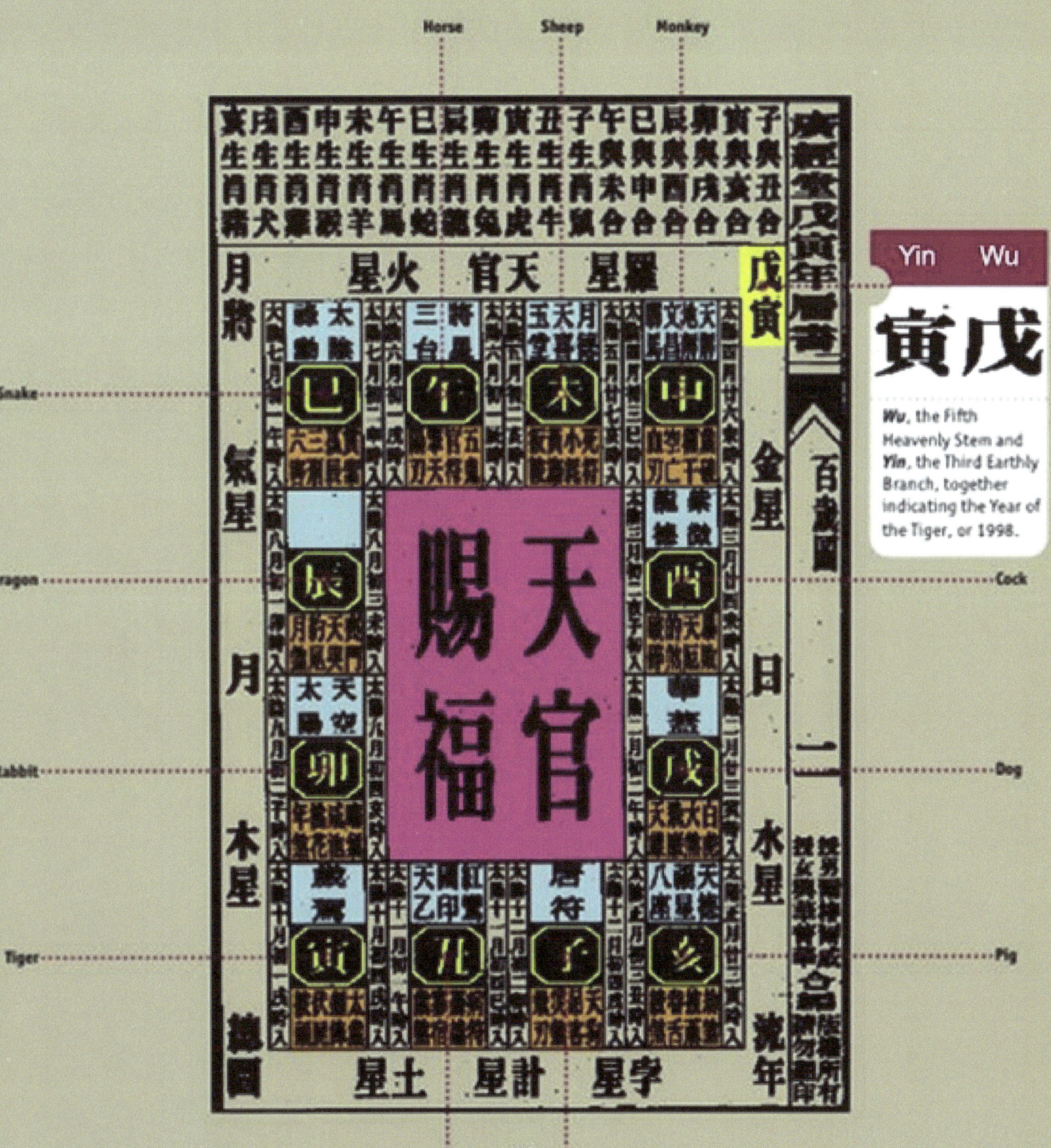

Yin Wu

*Wu*, the Fifth Heavenly Stem and *Yin*, the Third Earthly Branch, together indicating the Year of the Tiger, or 1998.

# THE CHINESE ALMANAC

## 4 a brief history

# Reading

By looking at the translation of the table and looking up your year of birth, you can see not only your Heavenly Stem and Earthly Branch, but also the 'zodiacal' animal for the year of your birth. It is the 'zodiacal' animal that most people associate with Chinese horoscopes.

**WE CONTINUE THE SERIES OF ARTICLES WHICH DECIPHER THE MYSTERIES OF THE CHINESE ALMANAC**

Throughout history, mankind has passionately sought to find an all-encompassing order in nature so that life on this planet could become more stable and predictable. This elaborate order often reveals itself as cyclical patterns of time and season.

The Chinese measure time differently to the Western calendar in so much as it is based on a mixture of the lunar calendar (moon phase cycle every 29.5 days) and the earth's movement around the sun throughout the year (ie. 365.24 days per year) and the consequent seasons. The yearly cycle in the Chinese calendar is known as the Sexagenary Cycle and revolves around cycles of 60 days, 60 months or 60 years. These cycles are highlighted in the Chinese Almanac and are made up of combinations of the 10 Heavenly Stems and the 12 Earthly Branches. Therefore, you will find that every Sexagenary Year is given one of the 60 year cycle combinations starting with the first Heavenly Stem (*chia*) and first Earthly Branch (*tzu*) and finishing 59 years later with the last Heavenly Stem (*kuei*) and the last Earthly Branch (*hai*). During the 20th century, the Sexagenary Cycle of characters began in 1924 with *chia tzu*, and ran to 1983, with *kuei hai* before starting all over again (see box copy). This means that this year (1998) is called *wu yin*, because *wu* is the fifth Heavenly Stem and *yin* is the third Earthly Branch and together they indicate that we are currently in the Year of the Tiger. Each year also corresponds to an Element, and in 1998 it is the Element of Earth (as shown on the previous page Almanac 3.

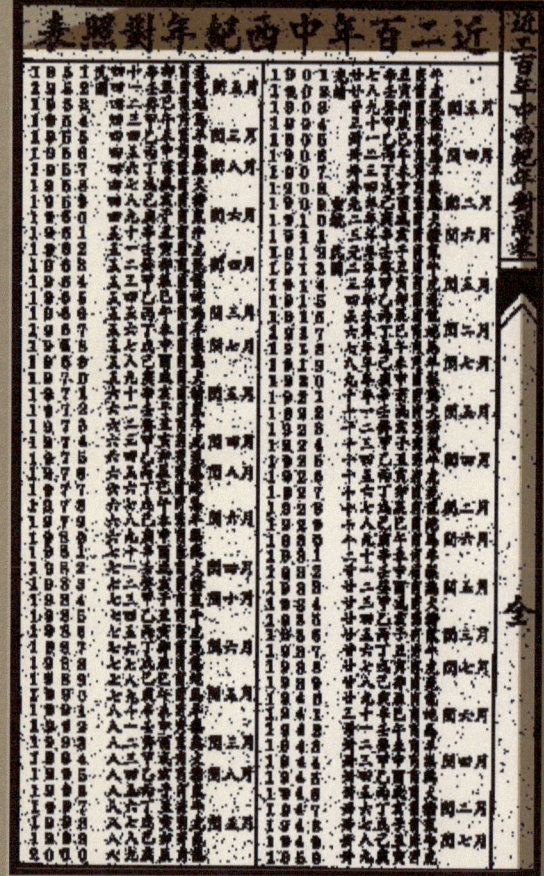

It is important to note that if you were born between 1st January and 20th February and your date of birth falls before the Chinese New Year (which varies from year to year) you should subtract 1 from your year of birth. For example, someone born on 14th January 1966 will use 1965 for these calculations because the Chinese year 1965 did not end until 20th January 1966. There are two other methods of calculating the beginning of the year – one is based on the winter solstice and the other on natural cycles, beginning the 4th or 5th of February each year.

# the Chinese Almanac

| Stem | Branch | Animal Year Of | Year | Element | Stem | Branch | Animal Year Of | Year | Element |
|---|---|---|---|---|---|---|---|---|---|
| Keng | Ch'en | Dragon | 2000 | Metal | Keng | Yin | Tiger | 1950 | Metal |
| Chi | Mao | Rabbit | 1999 | Earth | Chi | Ch'ou | Ox | 1949 | Earth |
| Wu | Yin | Tiger | 1998 | Earth | Wu | Tzu | Rat | 1948 | Earth |
| Ting | Ch'ou | Ox | 1997 | Fire | Ting | Hai | Pig | 1947 | Fire |
| Ping | Tzu | Rat | 1996 | Fire | Ping | Hsu | Dog | 1946 | Fire |
| Yi | Hai | Pig | 1995 | Wood | Yi | Yu | Rooster | 1945 | Wood |
| Chia | Hsu | Dog | 1994 | Wood | Chia | Shen | Monkey | 1944 | Wood |
| Kuei | Yu | Rooster | 1993 | Water | Kuei | Wei | Goat | 1943 | Water |
| Jen | Shen | Monkey | 1992 | Water | Jen | Wu | Horse | 1942 | Water |
| Hsin | Wei | Goat | 1991 | Metal | Hsin | Szu | Snake | 1941 | Metal |
| Keng | Wu | Horse | 1990 | Metal | Keng | Ch'en | Dragon | 1940 | Metal |
| Chi | Szu | Snake | 1989 | Earth | Chi | Mao | Rabbit | 1939 | Earth |
| Wu | Ch'en | Dragon | 1988 | Earth | Wu | Yin | Tiger | 1938 | Earth |
| Ting | Mao | Rabbit | 1987 | Fire | Ting | Ch'ou | Ox | 1937 | Fire |
| Ping | Yin | Tiger | 1986 | Fire | Ping | Tzu | Rat | 1936 | Fire |
| Yi | Ch'ou | Ox | 1985 | Wood | Yi | Hai | Pig | 1935 | Wood |
| Chia | Tzu | Rat | 1984 | Wood | Chia | Hsu | Dog | 1934 | Wood |
| Kuei | Hai | Pig | 1983 | Water | Kuei | Yu | Rooster | 1933 | Water |
| Jen | Hsu | Dog | 1982 | Water | Jen | Shen | Monkey | 1932 | Water |
| Hsin | Yu | Rooster | 1981 | Metal | Hsin | Wei | Goat | 1931 | Metal |
| Keng | Shen | Monkey | 1980 | Metal | Keng | Wu | Horse | 1930 | Metal |
| Chi | Wei | Goat | 1979 | Earth | Chi | Szu | Snake | 1929 | Earth |
| Wu | Wu | Horse | 1978 | Earth | Wu | Ch'en | Dragon | 1928 | Earth |
| Ting | Szu | Snake | 1977 | Fire | Ting | Mao | Rabbit | 1927 | Fire |
| Ping | Ch'en | Dragon | 1976 | Fire | Ping | Yin | Tiger | 1926 | Fire |
| Yi | Mao | Rabbit | 1975 | Wood | Yi | Ch'ou | Ox | 1925 | Wood |
| Chia | Yin | Tiger | 1974 | Wood | Chia | Tzu | Rat | 1924 | Wood |
| Kuei | Ch'ou | Ox | 1973 | Water | Kuei | Hai | Pig | 1923 | Water |
| Jen | Tzu | Rat | 1972 | Water | Jen | Hsu | Dog | 1922 | Water |
| Hsin | Hai | Pig | 1971 | Metal | Hsin | Yu | Rooster | 1921 | Metal |
| Keng | Hsu | Dog | 1970 | Metal | Keng | Shen | Monkey | 1920 | Metal |
| Chi | Yu | Rooster | 1969 | Earth | Chi | Wei | Goat | 1919 | Earth |
| Wu | Shen | Monkey | 1968 | Earth | Wu | Wu | Horse | 1918 | Earth |
| Ting | Wei | Goat | 1967 | Fire | Ting | Szu | Snake | 1917 | Fire |
| Ping | Wu | Horse | 1966 | Fire | Ping | Ch'en | Dragon | 1916 | Fire |
| Yi | Szu | Snake | 1965 | Wood | Yi | Mao | Rabbit | 1915 | Wood |
| Chia | Ch'en | Dragon | 1964 | Wood | Chia | Yin | Tiger | 1914 | Wood |
| Kuei | Mao | Rabbit | 1963 | Water | Kuei | Ch'ou | Ox | 1913 | Water |
| Jen | Yin | Tiger | 1962 | Water | Jen | Tzu | Rat | 1912 | Water |
| Hsin | Ch'ou | Ox | 1961 | Metal | Hsin | Hai | Pig | 1911 | Metal |
| Keng | Tzu | Rat | 1960 | Metal | Keng | Hsu | Dog | 1910 | Metal |
| Chi | Hai | Pig | 1959 | Earth | Chi | Yu | Rooster | 1909 | Earth |
| Wu | Hsu | Dog | 1958 | Earth | Wu | Shen | Monkey | 1908 | Earth |
| Ting | Yu | Rooster | 1957 | Fire | Ting | Wei | Goat | 1907 | Fire |
| Ping | Shen | Monkey | 1956 | Fire | Ping | Wu | Horse | 1906 | Fire |
| Yi | Wei | Goat | 1955 | Wood | Yi | Szu | Snake | 1905 | Wood |
| Chia | Wu | Horse | 1954 | Wood | Chia | Ch'en | Dragon | 1904 | Wood |
| Kuei | Szu | Snake | 1953 | Water | Kuei | Mao | Rabbit | 1903 | Water |
| Jen | Ch'en | Dragon | 1952 | Water | Jen | Yin | Tiger | 1902 | Water |
| Hsin | Mao | Rabbit | 1951 | Metal | Hsin | Ch'ou | Ox | 1901 | Metal |
| | | | | | Keng | Tzu | Rat | 1900 | Metal |

# THE CHINESE ALMANAC 5

# Reading

## THE 24 SOLAR DIVISIONS

**WE CONTINUE THE SERIES OF ARTICLES WHICH DECIPHER THE MYSTERIES OF THE CHINESE ALMANAC**

The next section of the Almanac deals with the subtle interaction of change in seasons throughout the year and the feng shui effect of this change. The 12 or 13 Chinese lunar months mark out the lunar cycle, the fluctuation of the moon from full to new over 29.5 days.

In contrast the solar year can be divided according to 24 roughly two-week periods known in Chinese as 'the 24 Joints and Breaths'. Each of these start on the days that the sun is either in the 1st or 15th degree of each of the signs of the familiar Western zodiac. This set of 24 always starts on 4th or 5th February with the *Li Ch'un* which is the beginning of Spring according to the Almanac. Although at this date the weather is still fairly cold in the Northern hemisphere, the Chinese maintain that the first signs of spring are visible in these weeks.

Some of the complexity of the Chinese feng shui compass comes about because of the need to relate the Heavenly *ch'i* to the Earthly *ch'i*. Earthly agricultural matters are measured by the solar calendar whilst the lunar is the sacred calendar measuring the fluctuation in Heavenly matters. In most compasses (*Lo p'ans*) the divisions of the 24 Joints and Breaths fall in one of the inner rings.

In the solar almanac the *Li Ch'un* is the real start of the agricultural year. Fortunately for us the dates of the 24 Joints and Breaths rarely alter (barring a day or so), and are therefore a much more stable measure of the agricultural year than the variable lunar months. This calendar was therefore called 'the farmers' calendar'.

The names of these 24 divisions are very graphic and describe the precise type of weather which would have been expected in Northern China at that time of year, as for example, the Beginning of Spring, the Coming of Rain, or the Great Snow.

It is important that the coming of the Chinese lunar new year (which fluctuates between 21st January and 20th February) is not confused with the *Li Ch'un* (the date of the festival of the Spring Cow), the start of the solar year which always begins on 4th or 5th February. Most Chinese festivals are calculated according to lunar year dates, but two major festivals, *Ch'ing ming* (the Ancestor's festival) and the Winter festival are determined by the solar calendar.

Here, we are considering the 24 solar divisions of the year which are basically agricultural and climatic. The full list is printed in the box, and each period takes 15 or 16 days.

There are also 24 basic directions, often referred to as the 24 Mountains, on the feng shui compass (3 subdivisions of each of the eight main directions) but they do not correspond with the 24 Joints and Breaths of the year.

Another interesting facet of the 24 Joints and Breaths is that the *yang* numbers 1st, 7th, 13th and 19th mark the start of the seasons, while the 10th and 22nd mark the solstices and the 4th and 16th mark the equinoxes.

# the Chinese Almanac

| Chinese Name | Translation | Begins - approx |
|---|---|---|
| *Li ch'un* | Beginning of Spring | 4th/5th February |
| *Yu shui* | Rain Water | 19th/20th February |
| *Ching chih* | Excited Insects | 6th/7th March |
| *Ch'un fen* | Spring Equinox | 21st/22nd March |
| *Ch'ing ming* | Clear and Bright | 5th/6th April |
| *Ku yu* | Grain rains | 21st/22nd April |
| *Li hsia* | Summer begins | 6th/7th May |
| *Hsiao man* | Grain filling | 21st/22nd May |
| *Mang chung* | Grain in ear | 6th/7th June |
| *Hsia chih* | Summer Solstice | 21st/22nd June |
| *Hsiao shu* | Slight heat | 7th/8th July |
| *Ta shu* | Great heat | 22nd/23rd July |
| *Li ch'iu* | Autumn begins | 8th/9th August |
| *Ch'u shu* | Limit of heat | 23rd/24th August |
| *Pai lu* | White dew | 8th/9th September |
| *Ch'iu fen* | Autumn Equinox | 23rd/24th September |
| *Han lu* | Cold dew | 8th/9th October |
| *Shuang chiang* | Hoar frost descends | 23rd/24th October |
| *Li tung* | Winter begins | 7th/8th November |
| *Hsiao hseuh* | Slight snow | 22nd/23rd November |
| *Ta hseuh* | Great snow | 7th/8th December |
| *Tung chih* | Winter Solstice | 22nd/23rd December |
| *Hsiao han* | Slight cold | 6th/7th January |
| *Ta han* | Great cold | 20th/21st January |

# THE CHINESE ALMANAC

## 6
### charms and talismans

# Reading

**WE CONTINUE THE SERIES OF ARTICLES WHICH DECIPHER THE MYSTERIES OF THE CHINESE ALMANAC WITH THE HELP OF WEI LOON SOO**

The use of the talisman or the charms (*shen fu*) have formed an integral part of traditional Chinese religion either for protection, or for warding off those evil spirits responsible for disturbing the delicate balance of life. A talisman or charm cannot simply be written by anyone or even photocopied. To have it properly constructed one has to seek the help of either a diviner, a Taoist or Buddhist priest or perhaps an astrologer.

The practitioner will write out the charm or talisman according to the needs of the person seeking help. The charms may be associated with one or other of the Chinese gods. The talisman is usually written out on a small piece of yellow paper using red ink with due reverence to the deities whose powers are being invoked. If you look at a talisman carefully, you will notice that the final stroke of the words are usually elongated and this is especially true for those principal charm characters whose final strokes are often further elongated into a twisting line. Such emphasis on the final strokes of the words is a representation of lightning which the Chinese believe can further enhance the power and effectiveness of the talisman. To them, the God of Thunder is a figure of order and correction who punishes wrongdoers by striking them with a bolt of lightning.

The talisman will often end in a style reminiscent of the former Imperial Edicts such as 'Let the Law be obeyed; let this order be respected and executed straightaway'.

The main form of talisman writing is that of Chang Tao Ling (also known as Chang T'ien Shih) who was born in 35CE. Legend says that Chang had a profound knowledge of alchemy, feng shui, astronomy and the *Tao Te Ching* (written by the great sage Lao Tzu) by the age of seven which led to the establishment of the school of practical or 'religious' Taoism in the province of Kiangsi. It is traditionally believed that when he ascended to heaven to become an immortal in 157CE, he left behind his seal, sword, a mystic book and a collection of charms which form today's Taoist charm and talisman study.

Take a look at the talismans and you will see that the inscription at the top of each talisman lays down the purpose of the charm, while the bottom sets out the method of using the charms effectively. They are usually stuck on the wall, hung around the neck, carried around in the pocket or burnt. Charms that need to be burnt usually involve the additional step of putting the ash into the water for later consumption.

For example, if someone is suffering from an eye ailment, the practitioner will write out an appropriate charm on a piece of yellow paper. It will be burnt and the ashes will be put into a bowl of cold water which will be used to bathe the eyes of the affected persons. For those suffering from abdominal pain, the ashes and water mixture will usually be consumed.

Many remedies are quite ancient, for instance, it was also quite common for pregnant women to drink the ashes from the bowl of cold water for the protection of their unborn baby. Those people who sincerely believed in ghosts or evil spirits, often affixed the talisman in the affected area to drive away the evil spirits.

# the Chinese Almanac

General incantation for use with talismans: 'The universe and *yin-yang* are wide, the sun comes out from the East. I use this charm to get rid of all the evils. My mouth spits out strong fire, my eyes shine out rays like the sun. I ask the Heavenly Soldiers to catch the devils and get all sickness out of this house. Heavenly Soldiers suppress evils and create luck. Let the Law be obeyed; let this order be executed straightway.'

To be carried whenever you move your bed

To be hung on the kitchen wall when you are installing a new stove - which is a key feng shui direction

Instructions for use of the incantation above - 'The person faces East and recites the following incantation, clenches his teeth three times, holding the water in his mouth, then spits it out.'

Portrait of Chang Tao Ling to show that these are an authentic talisman but such is his legendary power that this has become part of the charm itself

This charm is put on the wall to protect the home

To be hung on the main door to prevent the entry of wild animals

To be put inside a car or boat to avoid accidental loss

A so-called 'hundred different things charm' meaning that it covers everything and is a general talisman to prevent disasters

A talisman to place on a well to purify water and prevent disease (or burnt and thrown in the water)

Description of the purpose of each talisman

Instructions for the use of each talisman

25

# THE CHINESE ALMANAC

## 7

FOLLOWING THE CONVENTION OF 'AS ABOVE, SO BELOW,' CHINESE GEOGRAPHERS IDENTIFIED THE BASIC REGIONS OF THEIR COUNTRY WITH THE VARIOUS CONSTELLATIONS OF THE NIGHT SKY SAID TO RULE THEM. KNOWN AS THE 28 CONSTELLATIONS, THEY MAP THE YEARLY MOVEMENT OF THE SUN AND THE PLANETS AND ARE AN IMPORTANT PART OF CHINESE DIVINATION

The 28 Constellations occupy a prominent position in the elaborate daily listings in the Chinese calendar. The origins of the constellations are rooted deep in antiquity and are accompanied by a myriad of legends, but on a more practical level, the 28 Constellations, otherwise known as the 28 Lunar Mansions or *Hsiu*, are used primarily to determine the position of the Sun in order to make alterations and corrections to the Chinese calendar. However, it is in conjunction with the 24 Solar Divisions (see issue five) that the time of the year is accurately determined. For this reason, some of the original Chinese *lo p'ans* were inscribed with both these divisions.

Chinese astronomers identified the position of the Sun, Moon, and planets by reference to the constellations. However, unlike astronomers in the West, the Chinese divided the celestial domain into 28 divisions, all curiously irregular in size. The number of degrees allotted to each constellation differs. Such discrepancies however, are not due to inaccuracy and today's manufacturers of geomantic instruments cater for the diverse philosophies by providing a range of *lo p'ans* calibrated to the different systems. This is further exacerbated by the fact that old examples of the *lo p'an* are measured in Chinese degrees where the circle is divided into 365.25 degrees (days in the year), whilst the modern versions adopt the standard 360 degrees for convenience of reference. The reason for the wide variation of these divisions is probably historical. This may be due to the fact that the system of the 28 Constellations was not invented spontaneously, but was more likely to have developed over several centuries.

Adding to the difficulties created by these irregularities, variations can be found in the names of the constellations and the alignment of the constellations with the 24 compass Directions.

# Reading the Chinese Almanac

Each one of the 28 Constellations has its own constellation name, the name of the soldier hero associated with it, and whether it has a good or bad influence. The constellations are also linked with the five planets as well as the Sun and Moon which are further associated with the days of the week. (See pages 80 and 81, *Key Numerals*, for a more in-depth look at the 28 Constellations and their divinatory meaning.)

The 28 Constellations are further divided into four blocks of seven constellations each represented by one of the Four Celestial Animals, the same four animals at the heart of Form School feng shui, and their accompanying season and compass direction.

**Constellation** **Meaning** **Day** **Planet**
*Eastern Quarter – The Azure Dragon (Spring)*
1. *Ch'io* — Dragon's Horn — Thursday — Jupiter
2. *K'ang* — Dragon's Neck — Friday — Venus
3. *Ti* — Root/Floor — Saturday — Saturn
4. *Fang* — Room — Sunday — Sun
5. *Hsin* — Dragon's Heart — Monday — Moon
6. *Wei* — Dragon's Tail — Tuesday — Mars
7. *Chi* — Winnowing Basket — Wednesday — Mercury

**Constellation** **Meaning** **Day** **Planet**
*Southern Quarter – The Red Bird (Summer)*
22. *Ching* — Well — Thursday — Jupiter
23. *Kuei* — Ghostly Carriage — Friday — Venus
24. *Liu* — Willow — Saturday — Saturn
25. *Hsing* — Seven Stars — Sunday — Sun
26. *Chang* — Fishing Net/Bow — Monday — Moon
27. *I* — Wings — Tuesday — Mars
28. *Chen* — Chariot — Wednesday — Mercury

**Constellation** **Meaning** **Day** **Planet**
*Western Quarter – The White Tiger (Autumn)*
15. *K'uei* — Legs/Slipper — Thursday — Jupiter
16. *Lou* — Tether/Mound — Friday — Venus
17. *Wei* — Tiger's Stomach — Saturday — Saturn
18. *Mao* — The Pleiades — Sunday — Sun
19. *Pi* — Net — Monday — Moon
20. *Tsui* — Tortoise's Beak — Tuesday — Mars
21. *Shen* — Orion's Belt — Wednesday — Mercury

**Constellation** **Meaning** **Day** **Planet**
*Northern Quarter – The Dark Warrior/Tortoise (Winter)*
8. *Tou* — Ladle — Thursday — Jupiter
9. *Niu* — Ox — Friday — Venus
10. *Nü* — Weaving Maid — Saturday — Saturn
11. *Hsü* — Void — Sunday — Sun
12. *Wei* — Rooftop/Danger — Monday — Moon
13. *Shih* — Burning House — Tuesday — Mars
14. *Pi* — Wall — Wednesday — Mercury

# THE CHINESE ALMANAC

## 8

# Reading the Chinese Almanac

WE CONTINUE THE SERIES OF ARTICLES WHICH DECIPHER THE MYSTERIES OF THE CHINESE ALMANAC

This section of the Almanac is fairly lighthearted but it does highlight some important points. The page is divided into five panels, each one of which represents one of the Elements, counting from the top Metal, Wood, Water, Fire and Earth.

The strange heads sited like flowers on the stems of the plant represent the months of the lunar year. The blocks of Chinese on the left are poems which embody predictions.

How it works is that each year has a specific Heavenly Stem associated with it. You can determine which of these Stems represents your year of birth by referring back to the chart we published on page 85 of issue 4.

You will then find that each Stem relates to an Element as follows:

| | | | |
|---|---|---|---|
| *Chia* | (Wood) | *Chi* | (Earth) |
| *I* | (Wood) | *Keng* | (Metal) |
| *Ping* | (Fire) | *Hsin* | (Metal) |
| *Ting* | (Fire) | *Jen* | (Water) |
| *Wu* | (Earth) | *Kuei* | (Water) |

Using this table you can translate the Stem into the Element under which you were born. Next using this Element you can identify which of the five blocks on this page of the Almanac is relevant to you. Look at this block. On each head you will see a Chinese character representing the month number of the lunar year of your birth. The position on the plant then relates to the poem giving you your prediction for the coming year.

Let us take an example. Suppose you were born on the 13th day of the second month in 1984. The Stem for this year is *I*. From the table *I* relates to Wood. Wood is the second block down. Now look at the Chinese numbers on the heads. The highest head of the group in this block has two brush strokes on his hat, which is the Chinese character for two. Hence the prediction is the poem associated with this head.

We have not translated the poems as they are mildly amusing but not terribly serious divinatory portents for the coming year. The interesting thing about this section of the Almanac is the relationship between the 10 Heavenly Stems and the Five Elements, and the rather quaint head flowering plants used to illustrate the 12 lunar months of the year.

# THE ESSENTIAL GUIDE TO THE CHINESE ALMANAC

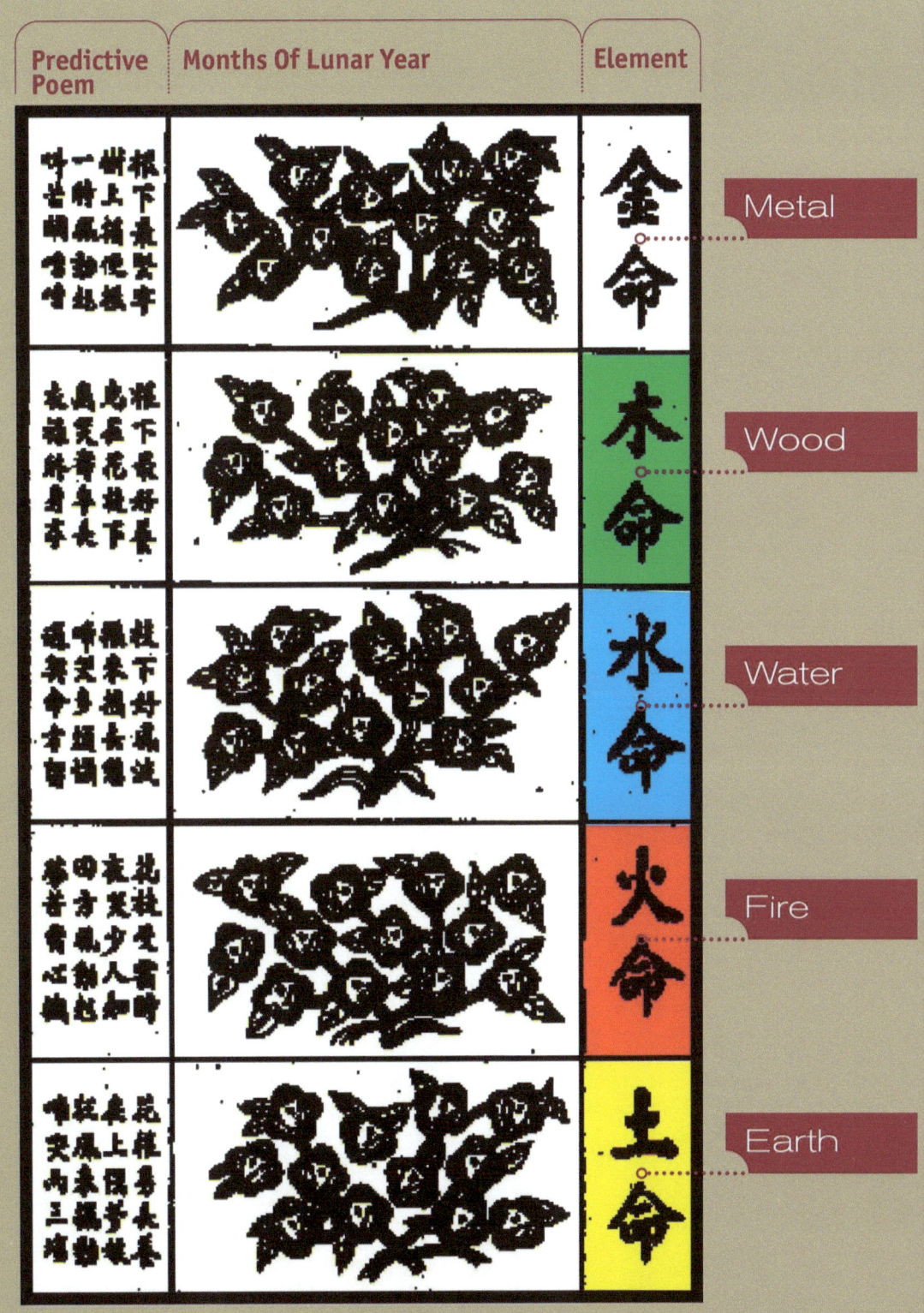

# THE CHINESE ALMANAC
## 9
### the nine planets

WE CONTINUE THE SERIES OF ARTICLES WHICH DECIPHER THE MYSTERIES OF THE CHINESE ALMANAC

This section is called 'Lighting Lamps' which has two meanings: the lamps of heaven or the planets, and the recommended propitiatory action of lighting five lamps to avert potential misfortune connected with these planetary influences.

There is nothing that points to the differences in Western and Chinese astrology as much as their respective treatments of the planets. Both systems traditionally counted seven planets, Mercury, Venus, Mars, Jupiter, and Saturn plus the Sun and the Moon. Uranus (1781), Neptune (1845) and Pluto were only discovered relatively recently. These three planets have been added in to Western astrology but have never been adopted by Chinese astrology.

A planet was by definition a body that moved against the backdrop of the fixed stars, and therefore included the Great *Yang* (as the Chinese called the Sun) and the Great *Yin* (as the Chinese called the Moon). It is interesting that here *yang* and *yin* are clearly connected to the world of light (day) and the world of shadows (night). For the Chinese, however, it was the backdrop of the 28 unequal-sized Constellations, which we examined in the October issue, that mattered most.

In the Almanac and in Chinese astrology generally, relatively little importance is attached to the planets. This is the exact opposite of Western astrology where the movements of the planets through the Zodiac, and the angles they make to each other on a daily basis is of crucial importance in drawing up a horoscope. Furthermore the Chinese tradition refers to each of the five 'real' planets (excluding the Sun and the Moon) as Elementary stars:

- Mercury is the 'Water Star'
- Venus is the 'Metal Star'
- Mars is the 'Fire Star'
- Jupiter is the 'Wood Star'
- Saturn is the 'Earth Star'

# Reading

Each planet is shown in this part of the Almanac in the form of its corresponding god or goddess. Each of these is thought to exert its influence over you in turn for one year at a time. In the Almanac there is a poem attached to each of the planets, which suggests how you will fare in this particular year.

The two columns on the left of the page relate your current age to the planet which affects your fate for this year. Bear in mind that the Chinese tradition is to count your age from conception, and therefore the following ages should have one year subtracted from them before relating them to your own age. Of the columns, the right hand column is for men's ages, while the far left column is for women's ages.

### Your Chinese Age This Year

**Sun**
- Men: 14, 23, 32, 41, 50, 59, 68, 77, 86, 95
- Women: 16, 25, 34, 43, 52, 61, 70, 79, 88, 97

**Moon**
- Men: 17, 26, 35, 44, 53, 62, 71, 80, 89, 98
- Women: 13, 22, 31, 40, 49, 58, 67, 76, 85, 94

**Jupiter/Wood**
- Men: 18, 27, 36, 45, 54, 63, 72, 81, 90, 99
- Women: 12, 21, 30, 39, 48, 57, 66, 75, 84, 93

**Mars/Fire**
- Men: 15, 24, 33, 42, 51, 60, 69, 78, 87, 96
- Women: 11, 20, 29, 38, 47, 56, 65, 74, 83, 92

**Saturn/Earth**
- Men: 11, 20, 29, 38, 47, 56, 65, 74, 83, 92
- Women: 14, 23, 32, 41, 50, 59, 68, 77, 86, 95

**Venus/Metal**
- Men: 13, 22, 31, 40, 49, 58, 67, 76, 85, 94
- Women: 17, 26, 35, 44, 53, 62, 71, 80, 89, 98

**Mercury/Water**
- Men: 12, 21, 30, 39, 48, 57, 66, 75, 84, 93
- Women: 18, 27, 36, 45, 54, 63, 72, 81, 90, 99

So for example a woman aged 31 *this* year will be counted by the Chinese as having an age of 32. If she looks herself up on the table above, she will find that it is therefore Saturn, or Earth, which influences her this year. The corresponding poem treats of her destiny in broad terms for this year. Likewise a man of 39 (Chinese age 40) will find that he is influenced by Venus, the 'Metal Star' this year.

# the Chinese Almanac

FENG SHUI FOR MODERN LIVING

**Ages for Women** | **Ages for Men**

- Sun
- Moon
- Wood Jupiter
- Fire Mars
- Earth Saturn
- Metal Venus
- Water Mercury

Water Mercury · Fire Mars · Sun
Earth Saturn · Moon
Metal Venus · Wood Jupiter

# 10

## The Chinese Almanac five coin prediction

These pages of the Almanac are concerned with the form of prediction which relies upon random throwing of Chinese coins. On each page there are six columns showing the various ways in which the coins can land eg. 2 'heads' and 3 'tails'. These are the same coins which are often prescribed as a feng shui Wealth cure when tied with red thread and attached to a till or cash book. You can see from the Chinese text that even the order of the coins is important as well as the number of 'heads' and 'tails'. This form of divination is used for answering questions about marriage, job applications and other business-oriented queries. Each throw combination has a poem attached to it giving the answer, which varies from the best possible outcome to absolute disaster.

Another more well-known form of divination which uses coins is the *I Ching*.

### Coin Prediction And The *I Ching*

In China, prediction by the use of coins has a long tradition. The best known use of coins in prediction is the *I Ching or Book of Changes*. The *I Ching* is a series of verses corresponding to 64 hexagrams, which are figures made up of six lines, one on top of another. Each line is either whole (*yang*) or broken (*yin*). These hexagrams are based on combinations of the eight Trigrams attributed to Fu Hsi, which are so important to feng shui.

The *I Ching* was compiled in the 11th century BCE by King Wen, the founder of the Chou Dynasty, who expanded it with more detailed commentary. After his death his son completed it with a commentary on each of the individual lines of each hexagram. Even Confucius wrote a commentary on the *I Ching*.

The *I Ching* is both a serious philosophical work and a working oracle. To derive an answer to a question it is necessary to first select a hexagram and then to interpret its associated verses as an answer. There are various ways of selecting the answering hexagram.

One method involves an elaborate casting of the stalks of the yarrow plant, which can take half an hour or more to derive the appropriate hexagram. Another method uses coins which is a far simpler form of this procedure.

When using the *I Ching*, adequate mental and spiritual preparation is essential to induce a receptive and meditative frame of mind in the questioner. Such preparation and an attitude of serious inquiry are vital to most methods of prediction, both in Chinese and Western tradition. First, incense is burned and the question which is to be answered is addressed directly to the *I Ching*. Before being thrown, the coins or stalks are passed through the incense smoke.

### The *Yin* And *Yang* Of Coins

The coins used for selecting the *I Ching* hexagram are usually ancient Chinese coins, which are circular with a square hole in the middle. The circle represents Heaven while the square represents Earth. Four characters are engraved on the *yang* side, while the *yin* side either has two characters or none. As it is believed that coins used for prediction will absorb influences from those who handle them, they should be kept separate and only used for this purpose.

Three coins are thrown six times in all to derive the six lines of the hexagram. The lines are recorded from the bottom upwards. Each throw can be either *yang* or *yin*. In addition each line is seen as being moving (that is changing to its opposite) or unmoving.

If the coins fall so that they show one *yang* face and two *yin* faces, this is written down as an unmoving *yang* or unbroken line. Three *yang* faces mean a moving *yang* line, that is an unbroken line tending towards a broken line (*yin*). Three *yin* faces, on the other hand is a moving *yin* (broken) line, and so on.

The hexagram is drawn up with the moving lines marked, and the interpretation of the hexagram read from the *I Ching*. The verses read from this hexagram represent the present situation. Each moving line is then changed to its opposite – ie. *yang* becomes *yin* and *yin* becomes *yang* and a second hexagram read. This shows the likely outcome, and reflects the idea that anything taken to the extreme eventually becomes its opposite.

# reading the Chinese almanac

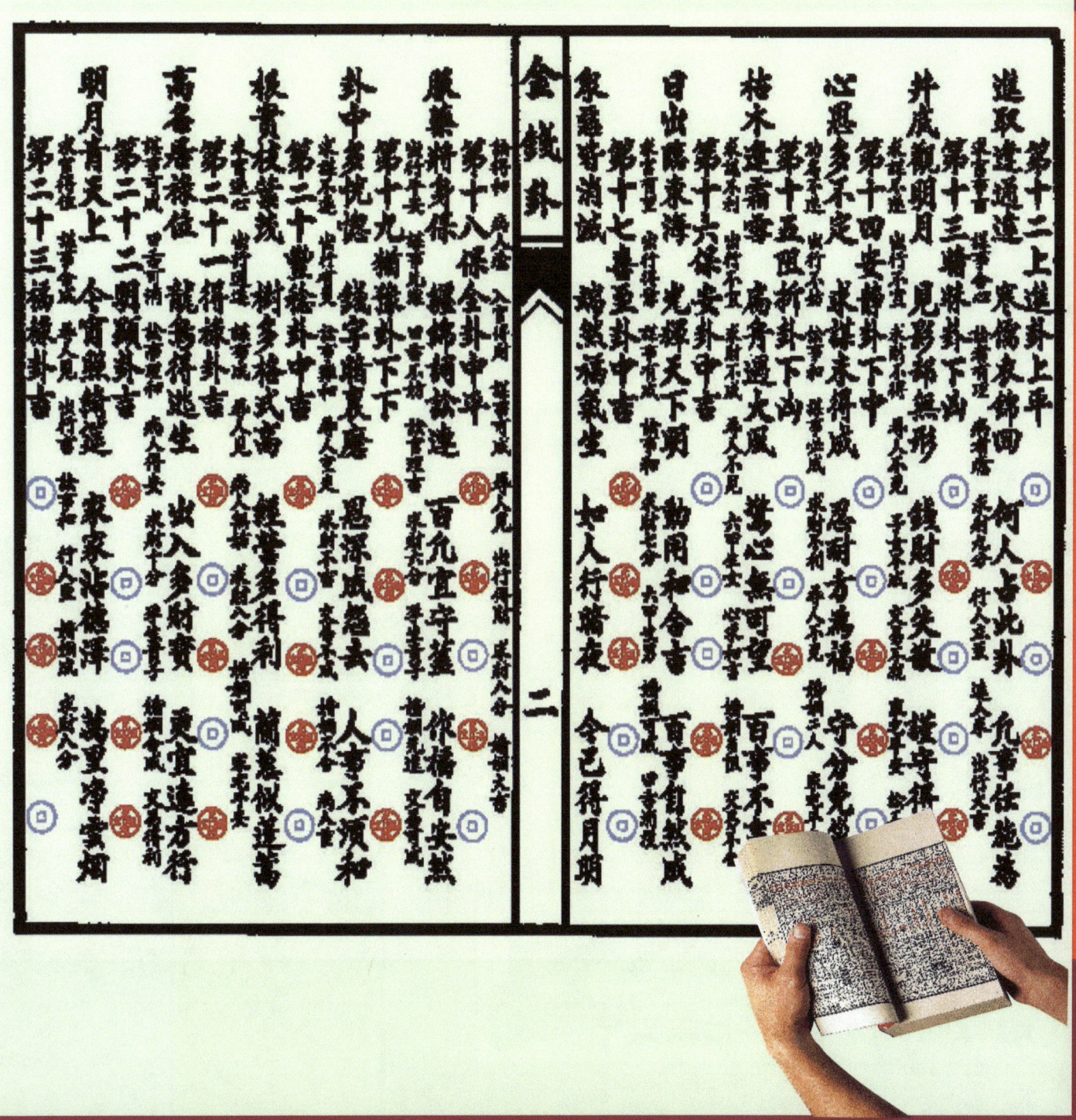

# THE CHINESE ALMANAC

## 11
### astronomy meets astrology

WE CONTINUE THE SERIES OF ARTICLES WHICH DECIPHER THE MYSTERIES OF THE CHINESE ALMANAC

# reading

The diagram on the far right shows the four Celestial animals, each of which is said to reside in a heavenly Palace. In order from the top of the illustration, the four Celestial animals and their heavenly 'Palaces' are:

| Palace | East | North | West | South |
|---|---|---|---|---|
| Celestial animal | Dragon | Tortoise | Tiger | Bird |
| Colour | Azure/green | Black | White | Red |
| Season | Spring | Winter | Autumn | Summer |
| Element | Wood | Water | Metal | Fire |
| Main star | Antares | ß-Aquarii | Pleiades | Hydrae |
| Chinese star name | Huo | Hsu | Tsui | Niao |
| Equatorial extent | 77.22° | 95.07° | 82.97° | 109.99° |
| Constellations | 1-7 | 8-14 | 5-21 | 22-28 |

Strangely these four quarters of heaven do not occupy equal areas of the heavens.

The astronomical pages of the Almanac include three distinct parts:

1 Explanations of the mechanism of eclipses, which is basic astronomy. Diagrams show how the eye perceives the shadow thrown by one heavenly body upon another, both for solar and lunar eclipses.

2 Four astrological illustrations showing the night sky for each of the four seasons, starting with Spring and ending with Winter. These conventional star maps are designed so that owners of the Almanac can identify typical star forms in the night sky. These are effectively scientific views of the sky with traditional Chinese names.

3 A diagram of the four Celestial animals which are usually associated with Landscape feng shui adjacent to a Northern Hemisphere polar star map showing how the four Celestial animals fit together round the central polar star and Great Dipper constellation.

It is the last in which we are most interested. At a glance the star charts in the main diagram do not obviously form the shape of the four Celestial animals, but these are outlined to make it easier to visualise the shapes. These four are called Celestial animals because they do in fact have a direct connection with the 28 Chinese constellations in the sky. The benefit of Heavenly influences can thus be related directly to the Earth. This is all part of the Chinese view of the Universe where Heaven affects Earth, and Earth affects Heaven, with man's fate decided by their interaction.

On the adjoining polar star map, the centre is occupied by the Pole Star or Great Bear, around which the seasons and night sky circulate. Embedded in each of these four Celestial animals are the 28 main constellations or *Hsiu*, which also show up on one of the outer rings of most *lo p'ans*. ◉

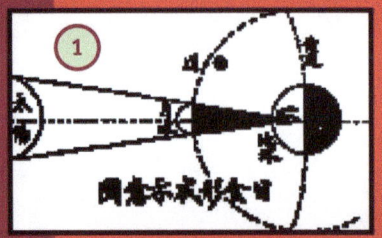

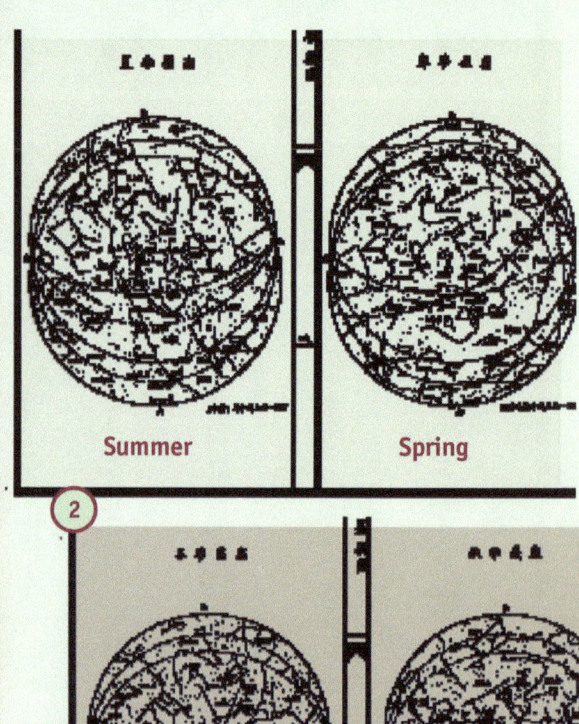

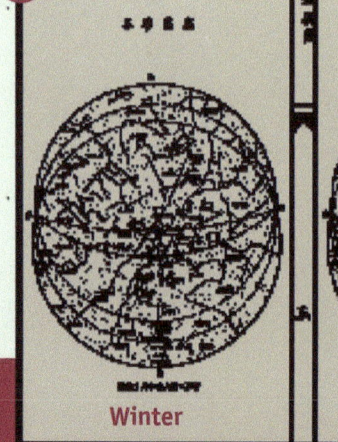
Summer

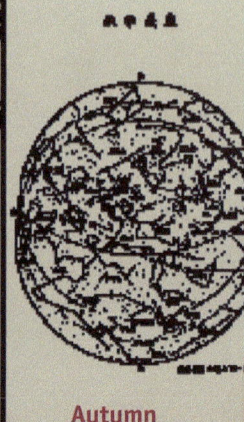
Spring

Winter

Autumn

# the Chinese almanac

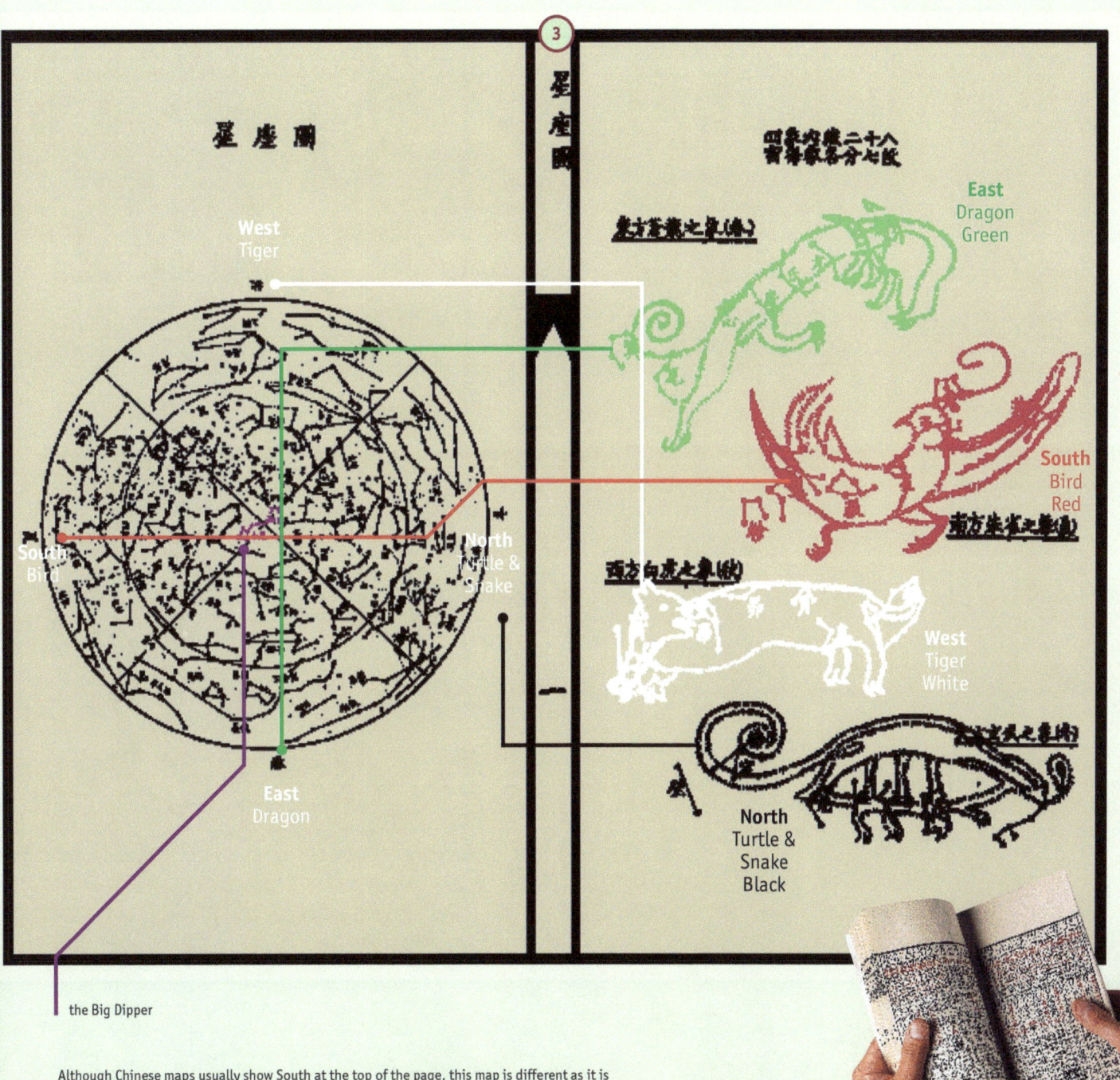

Although Chinese maps usually show South at the top of the page, this map is different as it is a view of the night sky from above the North Pole showing the different constellations visible in the Northern Hemisphere.

# THE CHINESE ALMANAC
## 12
### physiognomy, palmistry and fortune telling

**WE CONTINUE THE SERIES OF ARTICLES WHICH DECIPHER THE MYSTERIES OF THE CHINESE ALMANAC**

In ancient China, conceptions of the universe and natural phenomena were strongly influenced by specific methods of divination, also known as 'techniques of destiny', or *shu shu*, which were means of foretelling future events. Even though by Western standards these beliefs appear to be irrational and unscientific, they have nevertheless formed part of the cosmology of all Chinese thinkers through the ages, creating a link between Heaven and Earth.

While many of the Chinese divination tools relate more specifically to the celestial bodies and the earth's surface, there are other methods that are primarily concerned with human beings, such as physiognomy. This sphere of investigation is also known as *hsiang shu*, and is the belief that the fortune of the individual can be foretold by examining their physical characteristics such as facial appearance and bodily form. The Chinese believe that by reading faces, hands (palmistry), ears and bodies, they will know what to expect and, through their own efforts, improve their destiny.

Despite incurring criticism in the past from some of China's greatest philosophers, physiognomy and palmistry exercise great influence both inside and outside modern day China. In the annual Chinese Almanac, or *T'ung Shu*, both topics have a total of 10 pages devoted to them, consisting mainly of face and hand charts which map out the ensuing 12 months. However, the simplified nature of these Almanac charts means that those wishing to have a proper reading are better advised to go to a professional rather than rely on these charts alone.

### The Study Of Physiognomy

No one knows for sure why or when physiognomy and palmistry emerged in ancient China. One theory put forward by Hsun Tzu, a Confucian philosopher from the third century BCE, was that because of the chaos and uncertainty created during the period of the Warring States and the rise of the harsh Ch'in dynasty (475-221 BCE), people were looking for new divination and fortune-telling ideas to replace older traditional rites that had become associated with previous dynasties.

Although there is no doubt as to the antiquity of these divinational practices, there appears to be no mention of them in any of the Chinese Classics. It is in fact Hsun Tzu himself, a staunch critic of superstitious beliefs, who made the first recorded references to physiognomy in a highly critical attack, stating that, 'Formerly there were no physiognomists, and the word is not found in any books... Ignorant folks believed such nonsense, but in ancient times the practice was quite

# reading

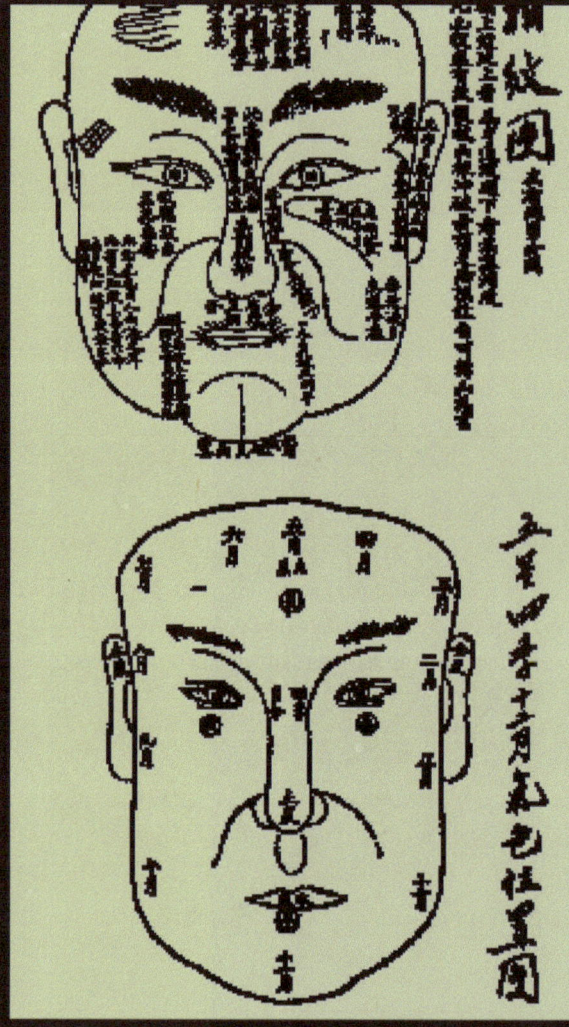

unknown...Therefore, a man's exterior, be he of high or low stature, gaunt or stout, gifted with fine features or ugly as a toad, exerts utterly no influence upon his good or evil fortune. The Ancients never noticed such twaddle...' However, Hsun Tzu's sceptical view of physiognomy never took root in the wider population.

Following on from these remarks, the principal works on physiognomy were not written until comparatively late, around the time of the great Sung dynasty (c. 960-1279CE). One of the earliest texts, the *Tai-ch'ing Shen*

# the Chinese almanac

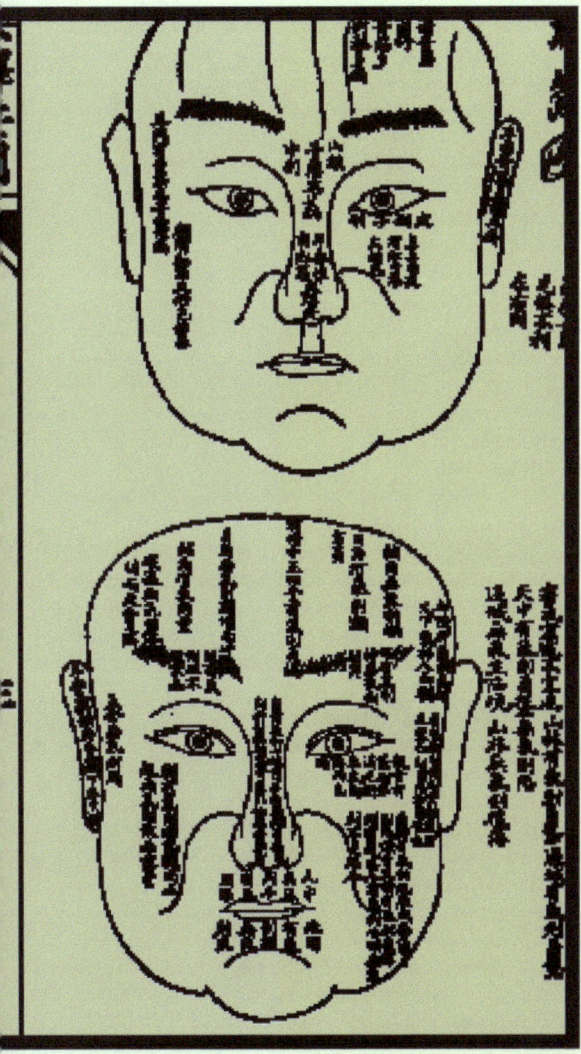

### A Hand Can Tell A Thousand Stories

A Chinese palmist can tell what a person's temperament and destiny is by the size and shape of their hands, with the more unusual shapes caused by bisecting lines indicating whether the owner will experience good or bad luck in their lifetime. As a general rule, it's the male's left hand and the female's right hand which are examined for information. It's also possible to determine what kind of vocation each person is best suited to by relating their hand type to one of the Five Elements such as:

**Hand of the Earth** – related to the qualities of Saturn, such as practicality and seriousness.

**Hand of Wood** – suggests something of resilience and endurance and is equated with the characteristics of Jupiter, such as largeness of outlook and expansiveness.

**Hand of Water** – associated with the Mercurian characteristics of quickness and versatility.

**Hand of Metal** – related to the qualities associated with Venus-like placidity, companionability and a tendency to be lazy.

**Hand of Fire** – associated with the fiery temperament and zest for life most commonly linked with Mars.

One way of checking an individual's annual good luck fortunes is by consulting the face charts in the Chinese Almanac each year, referring to the left side of the face chart for males and the right side of the face chart for females. It's not only the face and ears which the Chinese read, but the various bumps, scars and beauty marks, and their proximity to each other, in order to gain

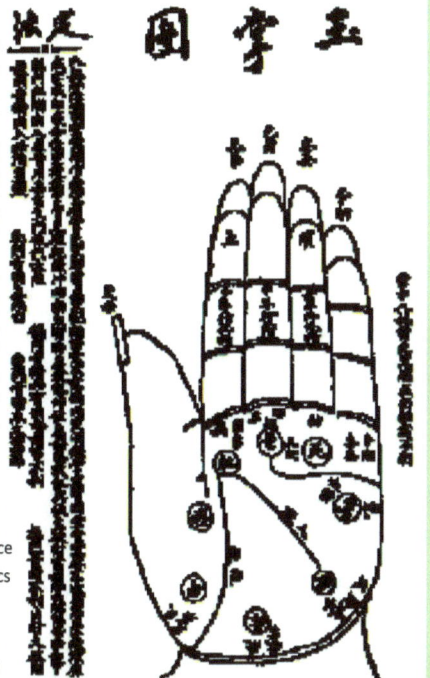

*Chien* (*The Mysterious Mirror of the Tai-ch'ing Realm*), said to have been compiled by Wang P'o in the sixth century but most likely completed in its final form during the Sung era, is still printed today, albeit in abbreviated form. The other major work on the subject, the *Shen Hsiang Ch'uan Pien*, was written in the 14th century by the physiognomist Yuan Chung-ch'e.

In modern times, the physiognomists' textbooks are full of highly detailed charts and diagrams, outlining all possible variations of physical features such as eyebrows, moles and ears. However, physiognomy is not merely concerned with facial characteristics. The discipline goes to great lengths to study the whole body including the weight, stance and shape of a person to give an initial impression, while focusing on the face to provide more detailed and specific information to complete the overall picture. From physiognomy and its offshoot, palmistry, the Chinese also came to the interesting realisation that finger-printing was an excellent and highly practical means of identification. ◉

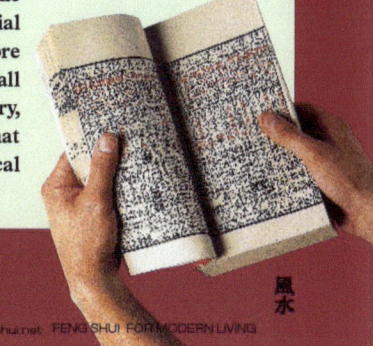

# THE CHINESE ALMANAC

## 13

### The main Chinese festivals

WE CONTINUE THE SERIES OF ARTICLES WHICH DECIPHER THE MYSTERIES OF THE CHINESE ALMANAC

The Chinese calendar can at first seem a little confusing to the Western eye. This is because it is based on both the lunar (Imperial calendar) and solar (farmer's calendar) cycles of time, whereby the moon determines the length of each month, while the sun governs the length of each year. Further to this, each day is made up of 12 double hours and divided according to the Five Elements.

The lunar calendar is the sacred calendar by which the majority of annual festivals are timed. However, because the number of lunar months in the year varies between 12 and 13, it is not of any practical use in understanding the seasons. Instead, farmers have used the solar calendar, made up of 24 divisions, to time the whole agricultural cycle. The lunar calendar on the other hand, focuses its attention on an individual's date and time of birth to provide the basis for astrological calculations which link individuals to specific fortunes. It is this connection between individual horoscopes and feng shui practice which, in fact, is a crucial determinant in finding a suitably auspicious site for a person.

The importance of this calendrical synthesis in Chinese divination and fortune-telling is revealed in the pages of the *Tung Shu*, or Chinese Almanac, which devotes 28 pages of its content to these time scales. The calendar itself is not only the oldest and most significant part of the Almanac, it plays a central role.

### The Festive Seasons

With its mixed black and red printing (denoting auspicious aspects), the calendar section of the Almanac carries details of all the major festivals throughout the Chinese year. They are featured in large vivid red printing on the actual day they occur (see the example of Li Ch'un, or first day of Spring, on 4th February 1999, featured opposite). Most of the major festivals are tied to the lunar calendar, and therefore the date on which each one falls changes annually, but not by much. Only three of them, Ch'ing Ming, the Winter Festival and Li Ch'un, are classified as solar festivals and thus occur on the same Western date each year.

### Main Chinese Festivals

All of the festivals have a specific lunar month date, but here we translate them to the appropriate Western dates for this year.

**Lunar New Year's Day**
**Month 1, day 1/Date: 16th February 1999**
This is the most celebrated of all festivals in the Chinese calendar. It starts on the first day of the lunar year, and lasts from seven up to 15 days. During this time of the year, children are given small red packets with money inside to symbolise luck, families gather to eat specially chosen food denoting good fortune, the Kitchen and Wealth Gods are 'received' into the home and, most importantly from a feng shui point of view, the door guardians are cleaned or replaced, depending on whether they are permanently fixed or made of paper. Firecrackers are used to scare off evil spirits, and the famous Lion, *Qirin* and Dragon dance through the streets.

**The Lantern Festival**
**Month 1, day 15/Date: 2nd March 1999**
The 15th day of the start of the lunar year marks the end of the New Year celebrations. There is much celebration and the festival is symbolised by the hanging of lanterns. This is a day when ancestral offerings are made and official notification is given to the ancestors of any new sons born during the previous year.

**Ch'ing Ming Festival**
**Date: 5th April 1999**
Ch'ing Ming means 'clear and bright' and is marked by visits to ancestral graves, which are cleaned, and paper and food offerings made. This is the major annual festival of the ancestors and quite significant in terms of *yin fung shui*. Ch'ing Ming is also one of the 24 Solar Divisions of the year and heralds the changing weather which comes just after the start of Spring. Paper money or 'Bank of Hell' notes are burned as an offering to the ancestors. 'Hell' does not have the same connotation as given to it by Christianity.

**Dragon Boat (Dumpling) Festival**
**Month 5, day 5/Date: 18th June 1999**
The fifth day of the fifth month is considered to be a dangerous day in the Dragon month. Celebrated with rice dumplings, its historical background is based on the life of Ch'u Yuen, a much-loved, and very honest, minister in the Kingdom of Chu (328BCE), who protested to the greedy emperor that his people were living in hardship. The emperor refused to listen to Ch'u Yuen's pleas and in a last ditch attempt to make the emperor realise the consequences of his actions, Ch'u Yuen drowned himself in a lake. While fishermen tried to save him, dumplings were thrown into the river to appease the water dragons in the vain hope that they would let Ch'u Yuen out of their clutches. So now dumplings and dragon boats are part of the festivities.

**Mid-Autumn (Mooncake) Festival**
**Month 8, day 15/Date: 24th September 1999**
Observing the moon, eating moon-cakes and reading hidden messages underneath each one, drinking tea and holding lantern exhibitions form part of this festival. During this time, the moon is at its brightest. People also try to see the rabbit on the moon because according to legend, the rabbit sacrificed himself for the Buddha who in turn granted the rabbit the moon as his home. A significant part of the story in this, the year of the Rabbit. Many of the procession lanterns are, for this reason, rabbit-shaped.

FENG SHUI FOR MODERN LIVING

# reading the Chinese almanac

**Left, top to bottom** Ceremonial offerings are made in Chinese temples throughout the world at times of major festivals.

Thursday, 4th February 1999

Li Ch'un or start of Spring

**Below right** 'Bank of Hell' notes burned ritually in the temple to ensure that ancestors' 'bank accounts' are regularly topped up with fresh funds

**Chung Yang Festival**
**(Double Ninth Festival or Climbing The Heights)**
**Month 9, day 9/Date: 17th October 1999**

The ninth day of the ninth month is particularly good for picnics, especially on hills and mountains, hence the requirement of 'Climbing The Heights'. Picnics held on high points are usually accompanied by chrysanthemum wine and special cake. Those who eat it at the top hope for advancement at work. The Chung Yang Festival is another day, alongside Ch'ing Ming, for visiting ancestral graves.

**Ancestral Memorial Day (Li Tung)**
**Month 10, day 1/Date: 8th November 1999**

Li Tung heralds the beginning of Winter. It's a day for families to remember their ancestors, perhaps by visiting a clan temple.

**Winter Solstice Festival (or T'ung Chih)**
**Date: 22nd December 1999**

This is a major event, standing alongside New Year in importance, and always falls on the Winter Solstice. Therefore, like Ch'ing Ming and Li Ch'un, it is one of the 24 solar divisions of the year whose date never alters as far as the Western calendar is concerned. The festival is the time for families to gather to honour their living ancestors as well as to enjoy a food feast, including symbolic glutinous rice-flour balls.

**Li Ch'un (Spring)/Date: 4th February 2000**

Li Ch'un is the start of Spring and, as a solar festival, it occurs on the 4th or 5th of February each year, rather than being attached to a 'moving' lunar date. It is the very first of the 24 Joints and Breaths of the year. This is the official start of the year so far as astrology is concerned. It also marks the start of the farmer's year.

# THE CHINESE ALMANAC 14

## The Core Of The Almanac

WE CONTINUE THE SERIES OF ARTICLES WHICH DECIPHER THE MYSTERIES OF THE CHINESE ALMANAC

The Almanac, known as the *Tung Shu* – or the Book of Myriad Things, has a history as long as 2250 years before Christ. It is a book that has had a much greater influence over the lives of Chinese people than any of the Four Confucian Classics, and its popular usage has lasted alongside any mainstream religious and ethical doctrines.

The calendar is the most important part of the Chinese Almanac covering 48 pages. It has a lengendary history of over 4200 years, originally being a set of lunar and solar dates correlated by officials under Emperor Yao. It was believed that dynasties fell when the emperors' legitimacy was removed by Heaven, and that a competent and legitimate emperor would be correspondingly in control of the earth and seasons. The creation of the Almanac symbolised this control. As a symbol of power and authority, the calendar came to provide justification and legitimacy for each ruler as the 'son of Heaven' throughout Chinese history. Therefore the compilation of the calendar has always been an important bureaucratic duty performed by senior officials in Imperial China. The last such Imperial compilation was done by the Bureau of Astronomy of the last dynasty Ching (1644-1912), although the calendar continues to be published annually since then in Taiwan and Hong Kong.

The calendar gives details of the lunar cycle and the seasons and it records every single day in the Chinese year. The original calendar was designed to aid agriculture, as can be seen in its information on weather, crops, sowing, harvesting, etc. As the Almanac was a product of an agricultural society where reliance on natural surroundings is significant and where the strengthening of family units is important to agricultual production, its relevance had to be constantly updated. Through the changes over thousand of years, in particular the last few hundred years when the calendar has received probably its greatest challenge, it has successfully accommodated to the needs of the time. A lot of categories in the ancient calendar are outdated and no longer in use, while some new categories have been added. Today the calendar is no longer just a day-to-day reference for the farming population, but is also widely used among urban Chinese as a direct reference for considering and planning work, relationships and for checking fortune and feng shui. This has made the calendar an essential guide for understanding the cultural practices of the Chinese.

### In the calendar, each day has eight main subdivisions within it:

**1** The Western calendar date including the day of the week, such as Thursday 1 June.

**2** The beneficial 'stars' on duty that particular day. The number of stars vary between two and four in number, except New Year's day which has six.

**3** The hours of the day, which in Chinese is divided into 12 hours. The calendar indicates clearly which hours are auspicious, which are average (*chung*) and which are inauspicious (*shiung*).

**4** The taboo activities, marked by the word 'to avoid', referring to the things you shouldn't be doing on this particular day.

**5** The Chinese date, including
a) the day of the month,
b) the Heavenly Stem (*T'ien-kan*) and
c) the Earthly Branch (*Ti-chih*),
d) the Element (eg. Metal, Wood, Water, Fire and Earth),
e) the title of the particular Constellation for the day and
f) the descriptive term for the day.
Those particularly auspicious days have texts on both sides indicating the most auspicious hour of the day as well as giving a warning for people born with specific Stem and Branch combinations.

**6** The suitable activities, marked by the word 'suitable' (*yi*). These activities along with those categorised as taboo activities, range from wedding, blessing, burial, travelling, moving, to placing beds, house cleaning, visiting, meeting friends. Under wedding, it may be suitable or not to buy engagement rings, have an engagement party or hold a wedding ceremony on that particular day. Under blessing, it may be a suitable day to place or set up a shrine. Under burial, activities include all kinds of arrangements for funeral services and whether it's suitable on a particular day. Under placing beds, it is indicated if the day is suitable or not to rearrange the location of the bed or the direction of the head of the bed for feng shui reasons. There are also special rules for a pregnant woman to relocate her bed during her pregnancy.

**7** This gives details about inauspicious 'stars'. The more stars here, the worse the day!

**8** This final category is made up of two parts, one is a title (two characters) giving a characteristic to the day, and the other is the rules governing building activities which shouldn't be undertaken on this day.

# reading the Chinese almanac

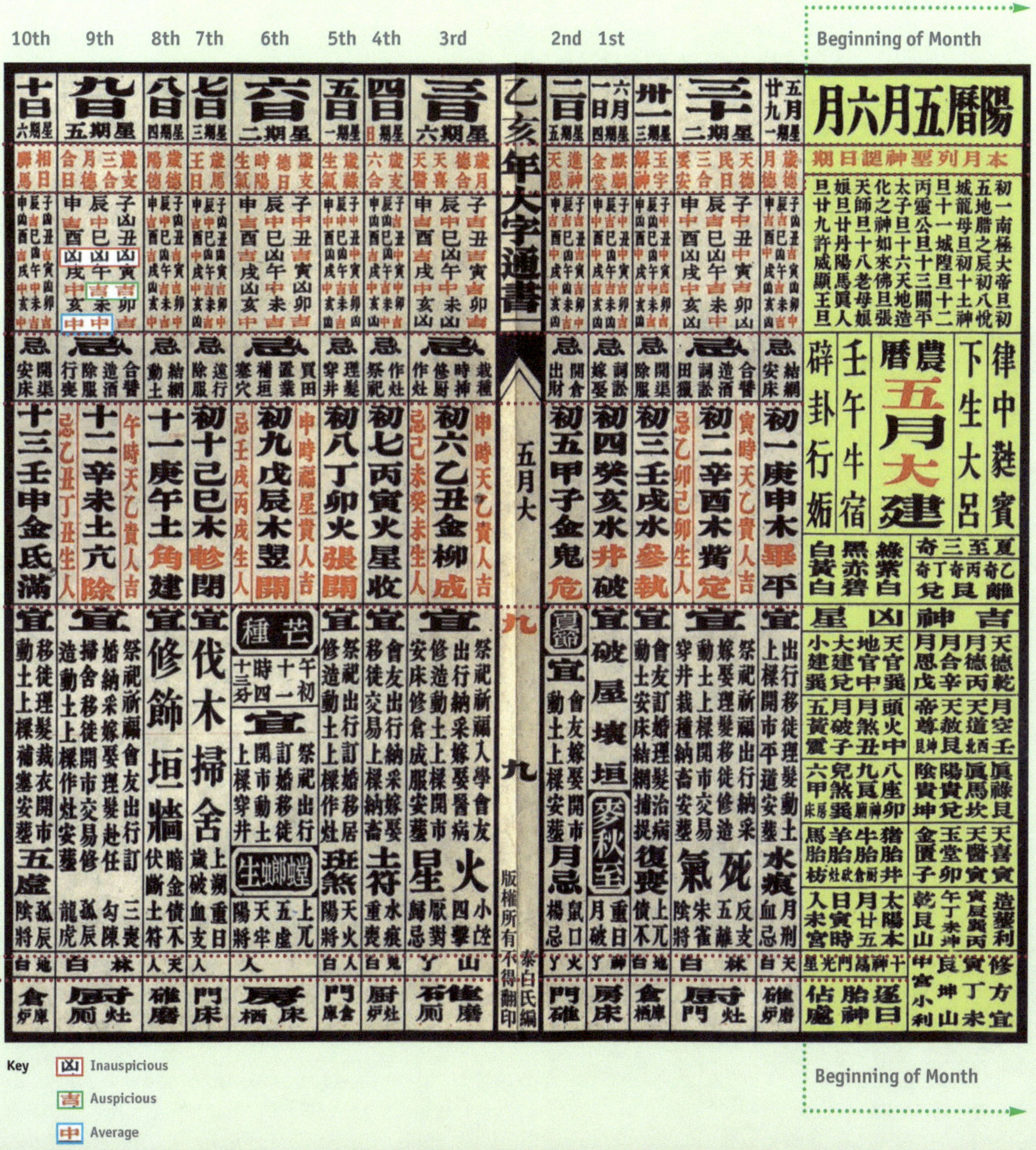

**Key**
- 凶 Inauspicious
- 吉 Auspicious
- 中 Average

# THE CHINESE ALMANAC

## 15

### The Core Of The Almanac

**WE CONTINUE THE SERIES OF ARTICLES WHICH DECIPHER THE MYSTERIES OF THE CHINESE ALMANAC**

Reading right to left, the first block at the beginning of each lunar month indicates the nature of that particular month. It is read like a detailed heading before you go into the contents.

One of the most important things people need to look up in the *Tung Shu* is the date of various religious festivals. The calendar carries details of all the major and minor festivals of the year. At the beginning of each month some of these festivals are listed. Some festivals such as the birthday of Kuan Yin, are more important than others. The major festivals are not usually listed in this block at the beginning of the month, but instead, are normally enlarged and marked in red print on the actual days of their occurence. Most festivals, major or minor, have to be recorded in the lunar calendar as their dates according to the Western calendar change every year.

### Guidelines For Daily Living

As well as festivals, the calendar gives practical day-to-day guidelines as to whether or not to engage in certain activities. Some of these activities are quite culturally specific for Chinese readers. For instance, ancestor veneration is seen as an important activity by the Chinese, and looking up the calendar to see whether it is a appropriate date for such worship is a very common practice. Many Chinese even have shrines in their own homes for ancestor worship. And of course, this is important from a feng shui point of view. The calendar is also used for checking dates for burial or changing the position of the grave. This is a particularly common usage in the feng shui-conscious Taiwan and Hong Kong. The position of the grave needs changing when the person's head is not pointing the right direction, just as feng shui has rules for the orientation of the living.

The calendar also suggests which dates to discard your old clothes, to have that really good wardrobe spring clean. For the Chinese it is important to renew your home environment and your clothes regularly, so as to bring in fresh energies, and reactivate your life. Every woman knows instinctively how important this is!

Some of you might wonder why even the timing of having a haircut matters in the Chinese calendar. For the Chinese, what you do with your body and hair is important to your well-being and to your relationship with your parents. As the Confucian saying goes 'our body, hair and skin come from our parents'. Thus the importance of having a haircut on the right day.

### Examples:

**A) 2nd June Friday:**
Of the 12 hours, six are fortunate, three are average, three are evil.
Outflow of money and opening of storage should be avoided.
It's suitable for meeting friends, getting married, opening a buisness and conducting a burial.
*Shia Jie*: summer holiday, the 2nd day of summer.

**B) 6th June Tuesday:**
Of the 12 hours, five are fortunate, four are average, three are evil. Buying of land, investment and repairs are to be avoided. The *Shen* hour is particularly auspicious, and you might meet people who could bring you fortune.
*Mang Chung*: month 5, sowing of seeds, best at 11:43 am. It's suitable for worshipping ancestors, travelling, getting engaged, moving to a new house, opening a business, changing the position of the grave, etc.

**C) 9th June Friday:**
Of the 12 hours, four are fortunate, four are average, four are evil.
Making soy sauce and wine, removing old clothes and attending funerals are to be avoided.
The *Wu Shi Tian Yi* are the particularly auspicious hours when you might meet people who could bring you fortune. It's most suitable for worshipping ancestors, praying, meeting friends, going out, getting engaged or married, having a haircut, taking up a new post, sweeping around your house, moving to a new house, opening a business, trading, reconstructing a building, cooking, conducting a burial and changing the position of the grave.

### At the beginning of each lunar month there is a special block of information which shows:

1. The Western calendar months.
2. A list of festivals, sages and deities for the month. Most of them are Buddhist festivals, and some are Taoist.
3. The Chinese month number and whether it is a 'big' lunar month (i.e. 30 days) or a 'small' month (29 days). Here it is a 'big' month.
4. Details of the geophysical characteristics and expected phenomenon for the month. For example are any floods or earthquakes predicted. It also includes the colour of the month and the influence it has.
5. This covers the names of the auspicious as well as the inauspicious stars for the month such as *t'ien teh ch'ien* (auspicious) and *yue sha chou* (inauspicious).

# reading the Chinese almanac

*Mang Chung*

*Shia Jie*

Beginning of Month

Beginning of Month

1
2
3
4
5

A
B
C

# THE CHINESE ALMANAC

## 16

### The Chinese And The Thai Almanac

**WE CONTINUE THE SERIES OF ARTICLES WHICH DECIPHER THE MYSTERIES OF THE CHINESE ALMANAC**

This idea of right timing and the rule of nature can be seen in a most interesting way in the horoscope sections of the Almanac. As you know, Chinese predictions of your destiny are usually based on the matching of your Heavenly Stems and Earthly Branches at the time of birth. The timing of your birth predetermines what you are. To show how widespread the Almanac is, here we have an example of both the Chinese and Thai versions of the Almanac. This section shows predictions which relate to the feng shui Earthly Branches.

The emperor was considered to be the 'son of Heaven' and a symbol of the balance of humanity (holding the balance between Heaven and Earth). The image of the emperor is still used in the Almanac today. It symbolises the destiny of humanity as determined by Heaven and Earth. Take a look at this picture of the emperor. Written on parts of his body are the characters for each of the 12 Terrestrial Branches.

On top of his forehead is *Ssu*, the sixth of the Branches.
On his left shoulder is *Mao*, the fourth of the Branches;
On his right shoulder is *You*, the tenth Branch.
On the left of his chest is *Shen*, the ninth Branch;
On the right of his chest is *Yin*, the third Branch.
On his left hand is written *Wu*, the seventh Branch;
On his right hand is written *Hai*, the last of the Branches.
On his left knee is written *Wei*, the eighth Branch;
On his right knee is written *Chou*, the second Branch.
In between his knee is written *Tzu*, the first of the Branches.
On his left foot is written *Shu*, the eleventh Branch;
On his right foot is written *Chen*, the fifth of the Branches.

You look up the year of your birth Branch and then from the picture select the poem attached to the picture which explains the predictions attached to these Branches. These change year to year. For example:

**Ssu (Snake)** 1905, 1917, 1929, 1941, 1953, 1965, 1977, 1989, 2001, 2013, 2025
If you are born on the head of emperor [as the Snake is attributed to his head], you have a strong will and are a natural hero. Rise and fall, you might gain or lose, you know how to defend or offend when necessary, and you are always content.

**Mao (Rabbit)** 1903, 1915, 1927, 1939, 1951, 1963, 1975, 1987, 1999, 2011, 2023
**Yu (Rooster)** 1909, 1921, 1933, 1945, 1957, 1969, 1981, 1993, 2005, 2017, 2029
If you are born on the shoulders of the emperor, you are capable and are always
ahead of people. You work hard for your family, and only able to lead a quiet life in old age.

**Shen (Monkey)** 1908, 1920, 1932, 1944, 1956, 1968, 1980, 1992, 2004, 2016, 2028
**Yin (Tiger)** 1902, 1914, 1926, 1938, 1950, 1962, 1974, 1986, 1998, 2010, 2022
If you are born on the chest of the emperor, your career falls before it rises. If you keep strong and strive, you will develop your potential. You can enjoy peace, happiness and family abundance in old age.

**Wu (Horse)** 1906, 1918, 1930, 1942, 1954, 1966, 1978, 1990, 2002, 2014, 2026
**Hai (Pig)** 1911, 1923, 1935, 1947, 1959, 1971, 1983, 1995, 2007, 2019, 2031
If you are born on the hands of the emperor, you know how to step back and how to move forward. Altruism and independence are your principles, you and your spouse are virtuous and you could be together permanently.

**Tzu (Rat)** 1900, 1912, 1924, 1936, 1948, 1960, 1972, 1984, 1996, 2008, 2020
If you are born in between the emperor's knees, you have a root in your destiny and you need not worry. Although you never get much help from your blood relations, you have peace and fortune in your mind and you will benefit from it.

**Wei (Goat)** 1907, 1919, 1931, 1943, 1955, 1967, 1979, 1991, 2003, 2015, 2027
**Chou (Ox)** 1901, 1913, 1925, 1937, 1949, 1961, 1973, 1985, 1997, 2009, 2021
If you are born on the knees of the emperor, your temperament is gentle and you dislike force. You start up from nothing and rely on your own intelligence, wealth is accumulated when the time comes.

**Hsu (Dog)** 1910, 1922, 1934, 1946, 1958, 1970, 1982, 1994, 2006, 2018, 2030
**Chen (Dragon)** 1904, 1916, 1928, 1940, 1952, 1964, 1976, 1988, 2000, 2012, 2024
If you are born on the foot of the emperor, your life is tiresome although you are talented. At middle age your achievement is not great but lays the basis; in old age you have children and grandchildren all around you.

# reading the Chinese almanac

**Chinese page**

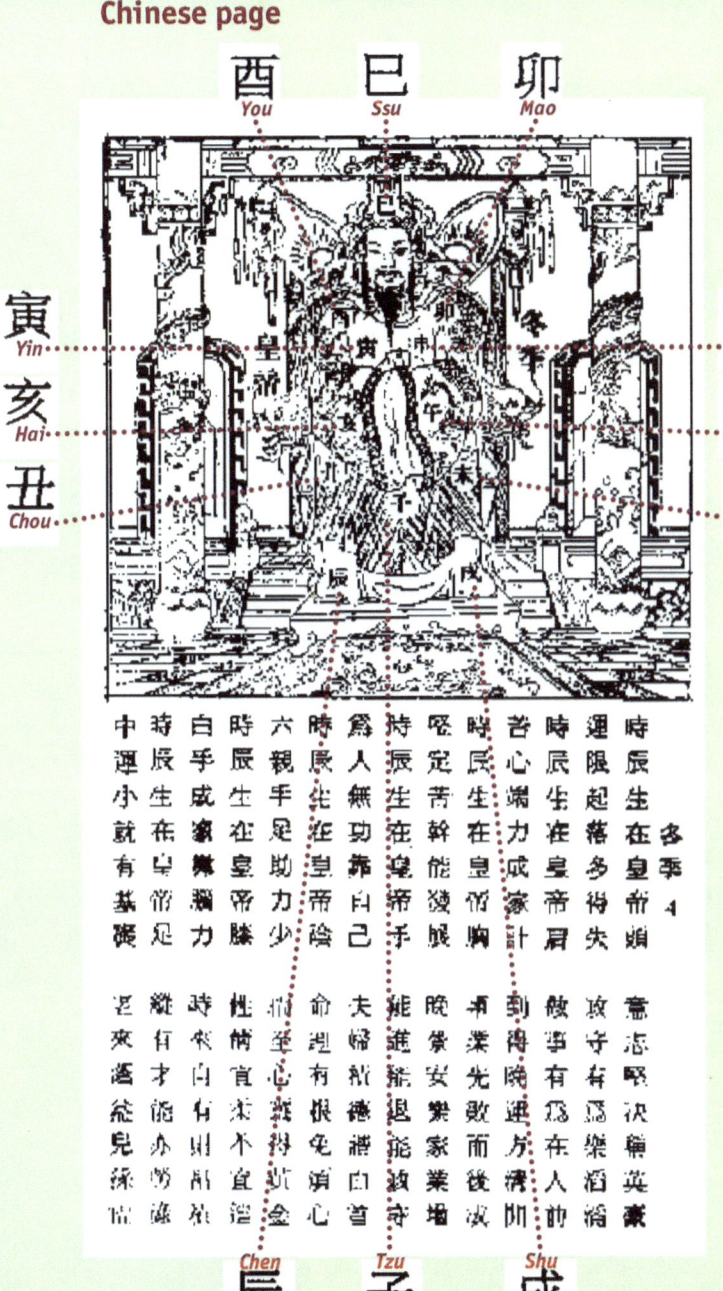

**Thai page**

# The Chi

## 17

THE ALMANAC HAS A HISTORY OF OVER FOUR THOUSANDS YEARS AND IT IS STILL IN USE TODAY. HOWEVER, THE FORM AND CONTENT OF THE ALMANAC HAVE CHANGED OVER TIME. IN THIS ISSUE WE LOOK AT THE ALMANAC DURING THE CHING DYNASTY, THE LAST DYNASTY OF IMPERIAL CHINA

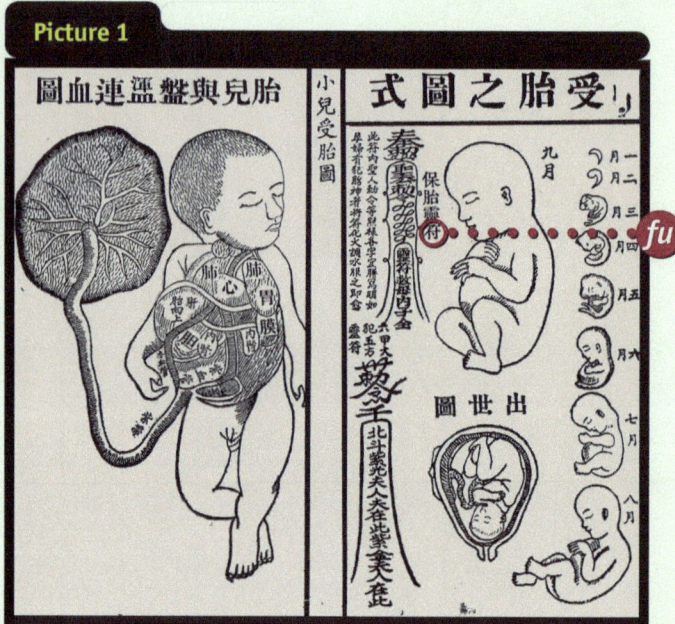

**Picture 1**

This is a picture called *Chu Shih Tu*, which means the picture of birth. It shows the size of a baby from one month old to eight months old. It also shows the position of the baby in the womb – seen as self-evident common sense now, but not so at the time of the Ching dynasty! In the picture on the right you can also see the character(*fu*) for the protection of unborn children. The script on the left shows how to use it: 'if a pregnant woman has offended the spirit of the womb, boil this *fu* in hot water and drink it, and things will be cured'.

In all Almanacs we can find day columns, diagrams and charts. But since the Ching dynasty, the Almanac began to differ from the past in many ways. First of all, it was no longer constrained by official formality. Apart from the standard charts and diagrams, its format relaxed a great deal so as to include woodblock illiustrations, numerous stories, poetry and prose. It was not only widely used but also popularised in its format. The cover of the Ching almanacs was no longer the imperial yellow but the popular and auspicious colour red. The variety of different names for the Almanacs also tell us that they were produced for different purposes, and for different groups of people, for instance, the merchants. Some of the Almanacs were used for the first time as trading manuals.

The Ching Almanac also differs in its content. It contains not only detailed information about the changes of four seasons, tidal movements and local times, it also had medical instructions on how to treat and recover from illness such as colds and headaches. There was also advice on pregnancy, ie. what women should do and eat.

The practicality of the Almanac also penetrated the private lives of ordinary people. This can be seen in the very explicit and detailed suggestions and advice given on the subject of sex. In the Almanac, sex was seen and treated as a very natural thing, where the point is to 'do the right thing at the right time'. Conception timing was important because it was associated with producing strong male children. Many Almanacs produced during the Ching dynasty, particularly at the end of it, recorded instructions on how to reproduce. This accords with the principle of the trinity, that balance can be achieved only through the timing of Heaven and Earth, in harmony with Humanity. In Ching Almanacs, it was understood that birth is not just a predestined process but one you can intervene in and make a difference by doing the right thing at the right time.

There was also advice on choosing partners and maintaining good marriages. While it was believed that the natal Heavenly Stems and Earthly Branches of you and your partner determine the nature of the relationship you are in, your efforts and what you do can also make a difference. This advice was given mostly in the fashion of moral poems and phrases, bearing some resemblance to proper Confucian lectures. They warned against excesses and encouraged a balance between one's spiritual and material/physical development. The purpose was to regulate the most private area of peoples' lives in accordance with the Way.

# THE ESSENTIAL GUIDE TO THE CHINESE ALMANAC

**Picture 2**

This is a picture called *Chiu Tzu*, meaning praying for (mainly) male children. The bold characters say, 'praying to Heaven and Earth for the continuity of the family line; praying to the kindness and benevolence of the gods; praying for the offspring of Dragon and Phoenix; praying for an offspring of literacy.'

The middle paragraph says, 'If born at the wrong time, there can be prosperity but no children. But if you are a sincere person and do good deeds, Heaven might endow you with a son of the Unicorn' (which means to wish for a good and successful son).

**Picture 3**

This is a picture called wine drinking (*yin chiu*). It is a depiction of a happy marriage. The text talks about the mutual affection, support and friendship between husband and wife. The middle paragraph says, 'a hundred years of happiness between husband and wife; drinking wine day and night through spring and autumn; abundance of food and clothing; good fortune shared in the household.'

The small paragraph on the left warns against adultery that would damage such marital harmony.

The text at the bottom is in Thai and parallels the Chinese text in this Thai version of the modern Almanac.

# The Chinese Almanac 18

IN THE PREVIOUS ISSUE WE LOOKED BRIEFLY AT THE CHANGES OF THE ALMANAC IN FORM AND CONTENT SINCE THE CHING DYNASTY. NOW WE LOOK AT THE DIVINATORY FUNCTION OF THE ALMANAC DURING THE CHING DYNASTY

Worshippers at the Lung Shan temple in Taipei line up for *ch'i* healing and to use the *ling chian* oracle sticks.

Ching Almanacs provided a number of techniques by which individuals could do simple divinations at home. One of the most popular involved an elementary system of counting on the finger joints called 'hitting the time' (*ta shih*). The nine finger joints are used even today by feng shui masters who want quickly to calculate Flying Star feng shui.

An example of a more mundane use of this is a quick calculation of the month, day and hour of an event to find out its outcome. This can be done on the six main joints of the three middle fingers of the left hand. First add in succession the numbers of the month, day and hour of a given event, so that you arrive at one of six possible outcomes to a question. An explanation is then looked up in the Almanac, predicting the outcome of the situation. Questions can relate to matters such as wealth, lost items, domestic issues (including marriage and pregnancy), travel, trade, illness, military affairs, and even litigation. A closely related but more complex technique of finger calculation divided the fingers of the left hand into 12 segments – four each for the index finger and small finger, and two for each of the middle two fingers. This would then give a more precise prediction.

Most almanacs also cater for the traditional yarrow stick divinations. Printed texts are used in conjunction with divining blocks (*chiao pei*) and 'sticks' (*ling chian*). Divining blocks were made of crescent-shaped paired pieces of wood or bamboo root, from three to five inches in length, with one side flat and the other rounded. After using the sticks, the blocks are used for confirmation. The blocks are dropped together, usually in a temple. They can fall in three possible combinations; both concave, both convex, or one concave and one convex. Based on these possibilities, a divination system developed in which various combinations of three throws yielded fixed answers to 28 sets of circumstances organised according to the 28 Lunar Mansions of Chinese astrology. As with the hand calculation techniques mentioned above, the most common categories of concern were money, movement, domestic life, health, lawsuits, and lost articles.

The sticks were a favourite divining technique of Chinese temple worshippers in Ching times (and are still very popular in Hong Kong and Taiwan). They came in sets that varied in number from 20 to more than 100 sticks. Each stick measured from six to 12 inches in length and they were numbered consecutively and kept in a bamboo tube. When someone sought to use them as a means of seeking guidance, they would shake the tube until mysteriously a single stick crept out of the tube and sometimes fell on the floor. The number of this stick refers to a text in poetic form. At most temples, functionaries helped people to read and interpret these oracles, but for those who could read, *ling chian* texts were often reprinted in almanacs providing explanations and elaborations. A typical example might suggest a good outcome with blessings and wealth or if you are involved in litigation your suit will receive a proper settlement, and so on.

*A modern set of yarrow divination sticks which are very popular in Hong Kong and Taiwan.*

WWW.FENGSHUI.NET

Typically the *chiao pei* crescent shaped divining blocks might be cast on one of the altars.

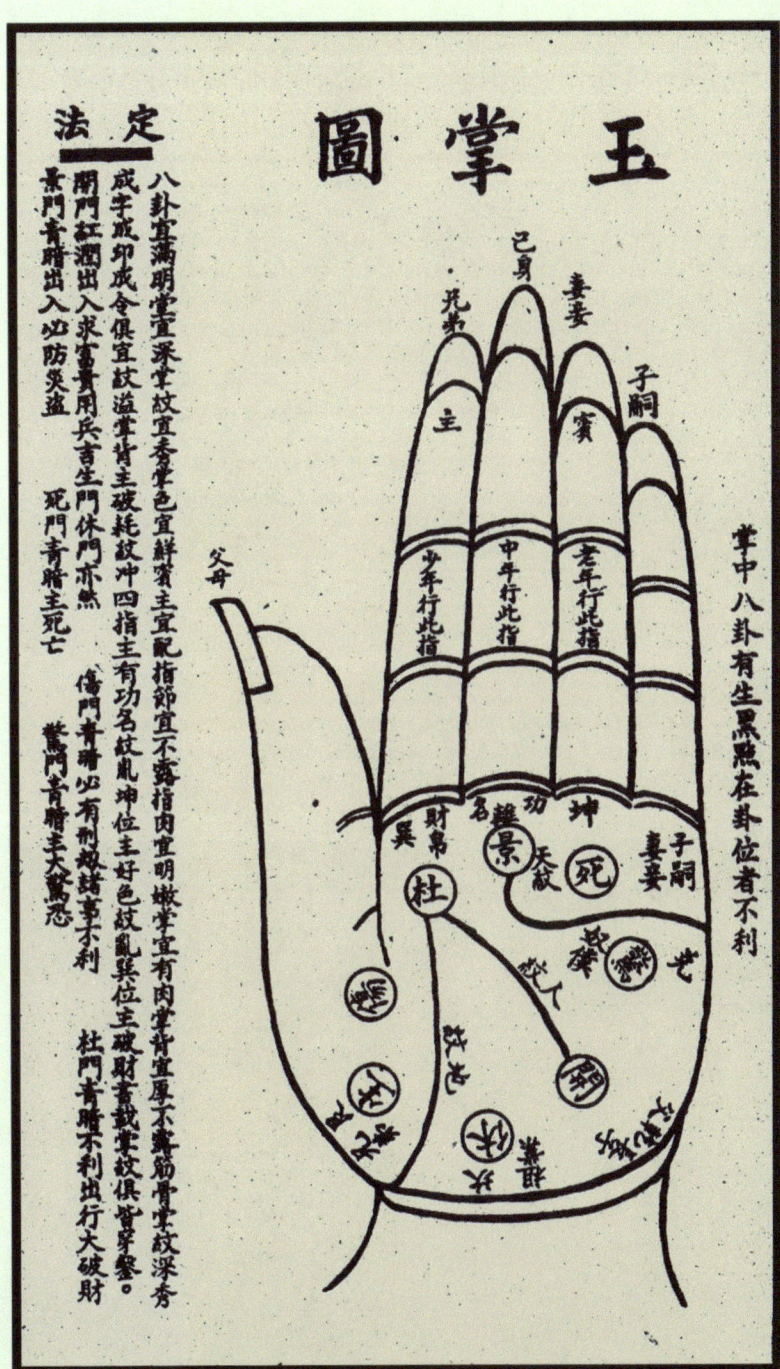

The eight characters circled are the life aspects in order from the top (clockwise) such as prospects, death, shocks, prosperity, fortune, births, injury and wealth. The characters on the left side are explanations of what these eight characters mean. Above the thumb is the character for parents, followed by other members of the family on other fingers – brothers (and sisters), self, wife and offspring.

### Personal Omens

In all walks of life, portents had enormous influence on day-to-day happenings in Chinese society so most Ching Almanacs offered a list of personal omens, which were further subdivided into a dozen two-hour periods defined by the 12 Earthly Branches. This secondary subdivision was necessary because the interpretation of each omen was also time sensitive and altered depending on the time of day. A typical list included:

- twitching or flickering in the eyelids
- ringing in the ears
- burning or itching feelings on face or ears
- quivering flesh
- palpitations
- sneezing
- clothes twisted or askew
- the bubbling of a pot on the stove
- the roaring of a fire
- a dog barking
- a magpie squawking

On the whole, Chinese Almanacs concentrated on favourable interpretations of omen texts, dealing with everyday occurrences and problems such as visits from friends, relatives and others, celebrations, and the accumulation of wealth. However there were also sections devoted to less favourable occurrences – accidents or injuries, disputes, legal matters, and, naturally, the loss of wealth. An example of the differing, but time sensitive, interpretations might be that a ringing in the left ear at the *chou* hour (1.00-3.00am) signified a quarrel, and in the right ear, a lawsuit.

Ching Almanacs were often a source of dream interpretations based on The Duke of Chou's *Interpretation Of Dreams* (*Chou Kung Chie Meng*) which, at its most extensive, consists of over a thousand dream divinations each condensed into a concise seven-character version. Again in the *Chou Kung Chie Meng* the majority of divinations are positive (such as 'When one rides a dragon up to Heaven, great honour will follow'), but around a third are more negative ('If the sun or moon descends from the sky, a parent will die').

It is interesting to note that in this influential work the recurring themes are a concern for good luck, wealth, health, high position, honourable children (particularly sons), and longevity and the greatest fears are death, illness, violence, poverty, lawsuits, and the loss of authority. Not only are these still of paramount importance in China today but can be considered global obsessions too! *Plus ça change*... ◉

# Chinese Almanac

## 19

### THE PLACEMENT OF GRAVES IS AS IMPORTANT TO FENG SHUI AS THE PLACEMENT OF HOUSES

In the Almanac you can find numerous references to *yang chai* feng shui (for the living) as well as *yin chai* feng shui (for the deceased). Yin feng shui involves examining ancestral burial sites with the intention of improving the feng shui of their descendants. For more than three thousand years, it has been believed that a good burial site will bring peace and prosperity to the offspring of the person so buried. The deceased were important in the way they influence their living lineage. Ancestor veneration was an integral part of the family values that have been central to Confucian ethics, but the feng shui practice of burial is a more pragmatic aspect of ancestor worship, as it effectively emphasises the interests of the living.

In looking at a burial site, the best fundamental configuration is, as many of you are aware, the 'armchair' configuration. The secure support at the back is crucial, symbolised by the Black Tortoise. As shown in the illustration, the Tortoise supports the site. As the characters at the back of the picture say, prosperity is generated for the children. On two sides of the site are the Green Dragon (East) and White Tiger (West), with the dragon side slightly higher than the tiger side. On the east side, the characters say, 'Wealth and prosperity in endless Spring'. On the west side, the characters say, 'An auspicious hsüeh (site) which is a doorway to good fortune'. In the South, the characters say, 'a wide and clear Bright Hall (*ming tang*)'. *Ming tang* also refers to the pool of water that Yang Yun Sung suggests should be placed in front of a site. The term is taken from the Ancient Book of Rites (*Li Chi*) and perhaps originally referred to a hall in the Emperor's palace used for religious rituals. In feng shui terms, the south of a site should have an unobstructed view (as the characters say 'all things pointing to the sky'). As shown by the illustration, the ideal shape of the *ming tang* should be semi-circle with one straight edge on the side, with the curve side away from the site.

As the text suggests, this hsüeh is auspicious because of its perfect armchair configuration. It gathers the maximum of beneficial *ch'i*, as shown in the middle of the site which is called *hsüeh chang* (site of dwelling). The text says that this auspicious nature of this hsüeh 'brings fame and glory to the offspring' and it would 'produce generations of high officials or powerful generals'.

However, the finding of an auspicious burial site has to follow the rule of Heaven, as well as that of Earth. Therefore, as the second part of the accompanying Almanac text shows, choosing an appropriate date to begin work is also absolutely crucial. This means matching the Heavenly Stems of the deceased person with those of the day chosen for the work. As the text says, carefully choosing the auspicious date promotes the building of the basis of family fortunes. And of course, this also depends on choosing a good feng shui practitioner to create the precise position of maximum balanced *ch'i* flow.

# FENG SHUI FORM SCHOOL

**Black Tortoise**

**Prosperity is generated by the site for the children of the deceased**

The best feng shui site (hsüeh)

後山高平　女兒山大貴丁

高清峰山

This configuration is an auspicious site (hsüeh) a doorway to good fortune

The wealth and prosperity of endless Spring

財丁興旺萬年春

穴場

專點吉穴福滿門

**White Tiger**

**Azure Dragon**

案山立案　主朝案軍　案開闊明堂

The mountains in front are a long way from the site　　All things point to Heaven (t'ien)　　A wide and clear Bright Hall (ming tang)

**Red Phoenix**

# Chinese Almanac

## THE PLACEMENT OF GRAVES IS AS IMPORTANT TO FENG SHUI AS THE PLACEMENT OF HOUSES

This Chinese map of a real landform is a classic armchair formation. This site is located near Taichung in the middle of the West coast of Taiwan, near the epicentre of the recent earthquake. The back of the site is supported by high mountains which form the Black Tortoise configuration, with layers of hills closely embracing it. The well-known tourist attraction Pa Kua Shan (Eight Trigram Mountain) is on the left. There is water running through in front of the site, with streams stretching into the area near the town of Nantou.

The point where most *ch'i* gathers is the *hsüeh* marked A. It is surrounded by inward curving low hills, enfolding it like the tentacles of an octopus. Imagine sitting on the tongue of land which is the *hsüeh* backed by high mountains and facing South across a picturesque river valley.

At B the Tatu River passes in front of the site with the water flowing from the source (C) at the right side of the picture. The river flows West in the direction of the water mouth (*kou*) at D where the river exits. On the original plan, the exit of the river is not traced because it is out of sight of the *hsüeh*.

At this point you can see the Chinese character *shui kou*. In Water Dragon feng shui, it is very important to identify the direction at which the water exits the site. It is also important that the water does not drain away from the site visibly, but disappears round a corner, thereby retaining the *ch'i*.

The triangle at E is the old village of Nantou which is now a thriving town in modern-day Taiwan. At F is the position where fortune and longevity accumulate to the site. Other increasingly named peaks include Pa Hsien Shan, or Eight Immortals Mountain, shown at H.

Another peak at I is called Treasury or Wealth Mountain and is a feng shui feature affecting the wealth of the site. At J Drum Mountain indicates a military influence. There is a pair of double mountains which are banner mountains at K.

Normally you would expect the mountain ranges to the South of the site (foreground) to be much smaller and rolling, but in this case I suspect the perspective of the original map-maker has compressed these mountains closer to the *hsüeh* than they really are.

As in most Chinese territories, burials don't always occur in a designated cemetery but can occur on private land. In this case the *hsüeh* is occupied by a tomb built with the intention of providing good feng shui for the descendants of the person buried. The theory is that the descendants of the patriarch buried here will continue through time to have good personal feng shui. Of course, this is only true as long as this site is not disturbed.

### THE CHINESE DESCRIPTION OF THIS SITE IS:

- The front of mountains are low hills
The *hsüeh* accumulates *ch'i*
(This will bring) glory to the offspring and descendants

- The air of the site is full of energy
The *Ming Tang* in front of the site gathers *ch'i*
The fragrance of the orchid lasts in the air

- The back of the mountains are high and far away
The height of the peaks and the auspicious *hsüeh*
Bring fame to the grandchildren (on the maternal side)

- The *Ming Tang* accumulates *ch'i*
The outflow of the water cultivates treasure
And will bring high rank in the family

- This points to a specially auspicious *hsüeh* which generates wealth for members of the family
The coming of water cultivates prosperity for the household
The construction of a *hsüeh* should be done at the right time
To bring fame to the offspring

- There is a modest person called Nan Yang who is the author of the *Tung Shu*
He is capable of examining the feng shui and pointing out the best *yin* site
A moral person should always get a fortunate piece of land
Bringing success and fame to the offspring

- Carefully choose the correct auspicious date to build a base for your fortune
(Which will bring) wealth to members of family for many years
To set up the gravestone you need to use the correct feng shui calculations
The offspring will then bring glory to the family

# FENG SHUI FORM SCHOOL

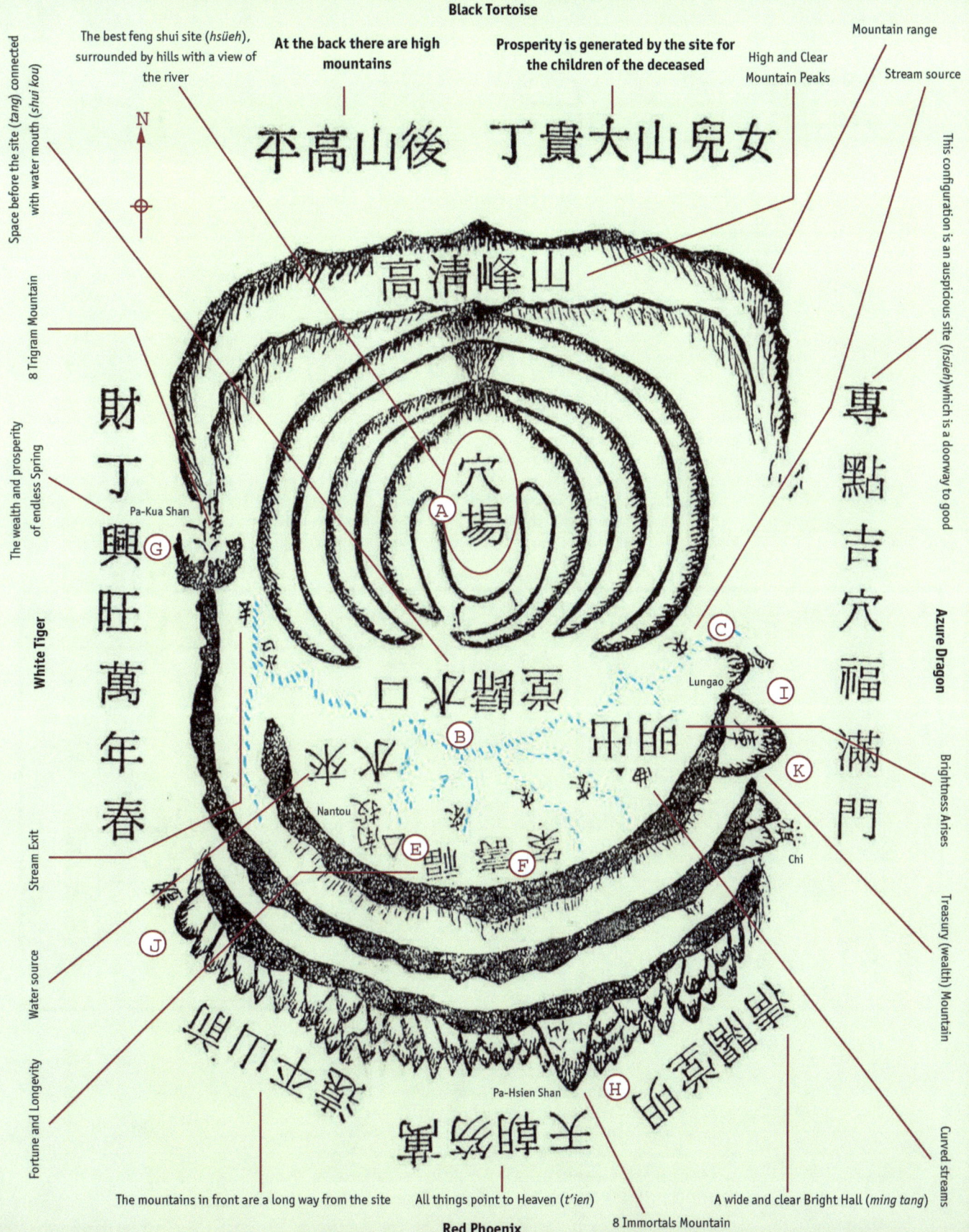

# chinese almanac

## 21

### THE FIRST PAGE OF THE ALMANAC FOR THE NEW YEAR

The year 2000 is the Keng Ch'en year. Keng is the 7th of the Ten Heavenly Stems. Ch'en is the 5th of the Twelve Earthly Branches. The combination indicates the year of the Dragon. Keng and Ch'en together make the characters for the year 2000.

This is the first page of the Almanac for 2000 which always shows a picture of the 'Spring Cow'. The picture changes subtly from year to year and it predicts the agricultural conditions for the coming year. Compared to the Spring Cow picture of last year, the farmer depicted here is wearing less and the sun is stronger. This means it will be a warmer year. He is not wearing a hat so heavy rains are not predicted. The Spring Cow picture therefore gives the impression that there will be droughts this year. The description of the Spring Cow picture reads, 'Tai Sui is on Keng Ch'en this year. The dragon head appears in Tung Chin. Disasters may harm cattle. Diseases may harm people.' The Spring Cow picture and its text is entirely for agricultural use. It predicts the weather, farming and harvest prospects. It gives very detailed information such as weather for particular days. For example, the fifteenth of the first lunar month (7 February) will be a rainy day. And the 24th of the seventh lunar month (11 September) will be a very warm day. Each (lunar) month is marked as a 'big' or 'small' month according to the number of days in it. The whole page is an interesting confirmation of how the almanac was originally used as a farming calendar.

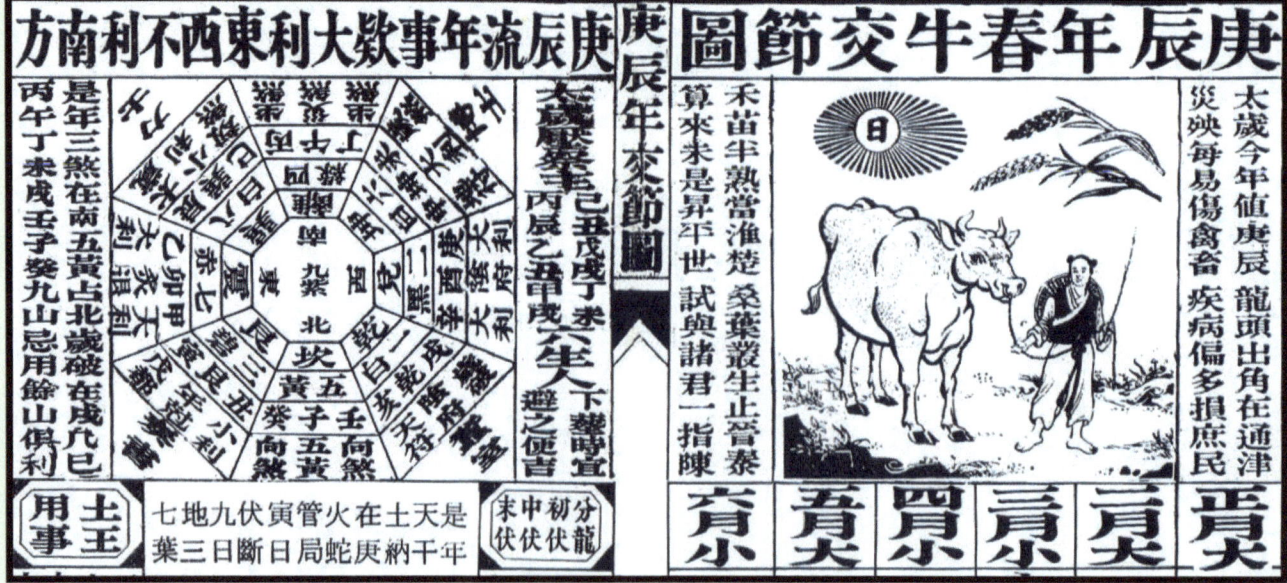

The chart on the left shows feng shui Flying Star locations and directions for the year 2000. The characters on top say, 'East and West are beneficial; the South is not.' The Flying Stars each have a number and colour associated with them, and position every year. For example the number 5 is ideally to be found in the centre of the *lo shu* square and is called Five Yellow (*wu huang*). Its element is Earth. Another example is the Nine Purple Star (*Chiu tzu*), which ideally should be in the South. This year unfortunately the Five Yellow falls in the North, with Nine Purple in the centre. This makes it not a very fortunate year.

# FENG SHUI FOR MODERN LIVING

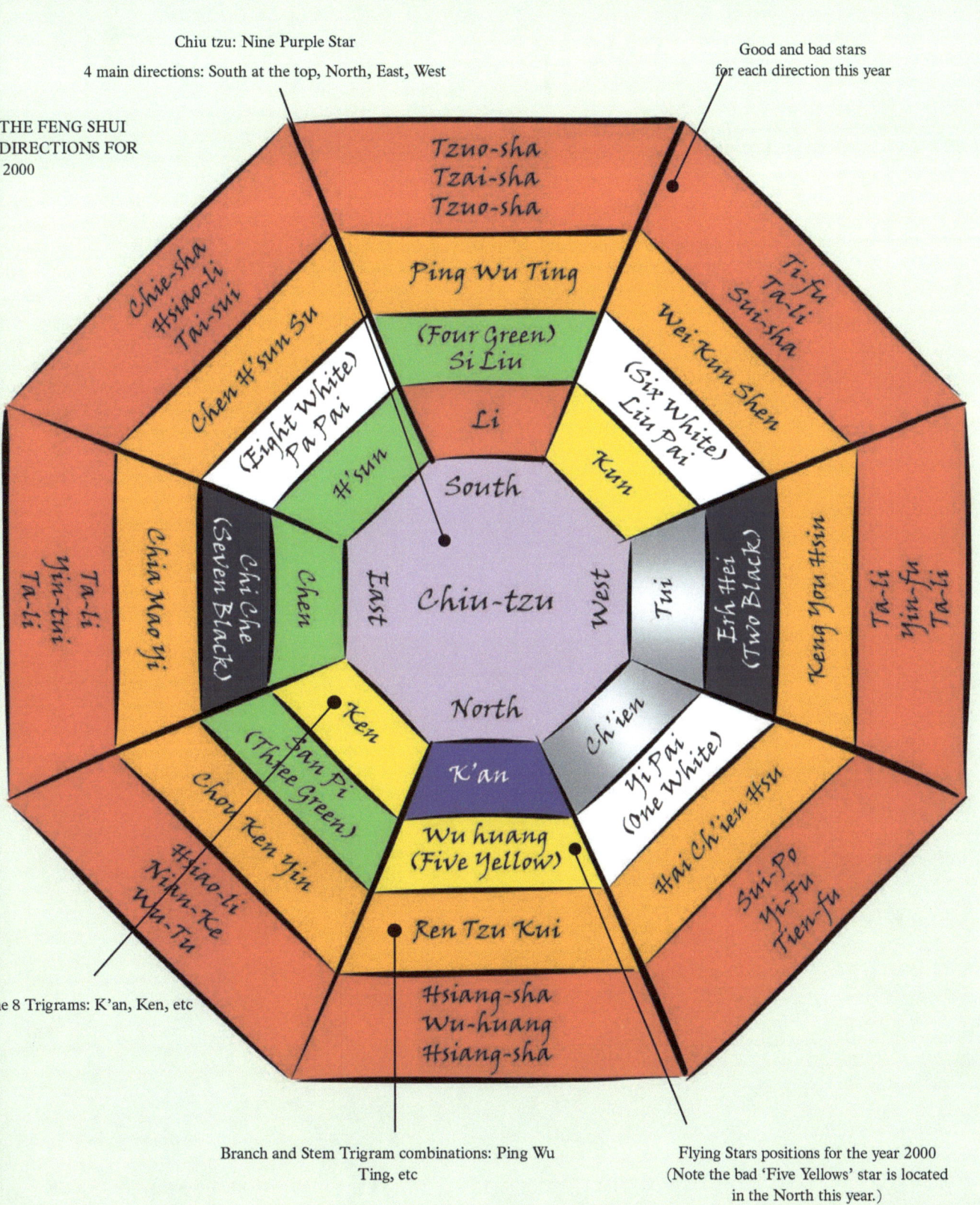

# Chinese Almanac   22

IN ALL THE PREVIOUS CHAPTERS WE HAVE TALKED ABOUT HOW THE CHINESE ALMANAC HAS ALWAYS BEEN AN ESSENTIAL PART OF THE THEORY AND PRACTICE OF FENG SHUI. HERE WE LOOK AT HOW THE TWENTY-EIGHT CONSTELLATIONS (*HSIU*) OR LUNAR MANSIONS ARE AN INTEGRAL PART OF THE ALMANAC AND THE FENG SHUI COMPASS

In Chinese astrology, each day of our lives is attributed to a constellation (*hsiu*). A constellation defines the auspicious or inauspicious nature of a particular day. There are twenty-eight constellations because the moon takes approximately 28 days to complete its cycle. These can be clearly divided by four so that each constellation would always return on the same day of the week. These twenty-eight *hsiu* were originally used to determine the position of the Sun in order to make corrections to the calendar, and to calculate eclipses. The twenty-eight constellations are however spectacularly irregular in size, ranging from just one degree (*tsui*) to 31 degrees (*ching*).

Each of the twenty-eight constellations has its own prediction given in the Almanac. Some of them might seem completely outdated and very draconian. However, they are

卯 East point

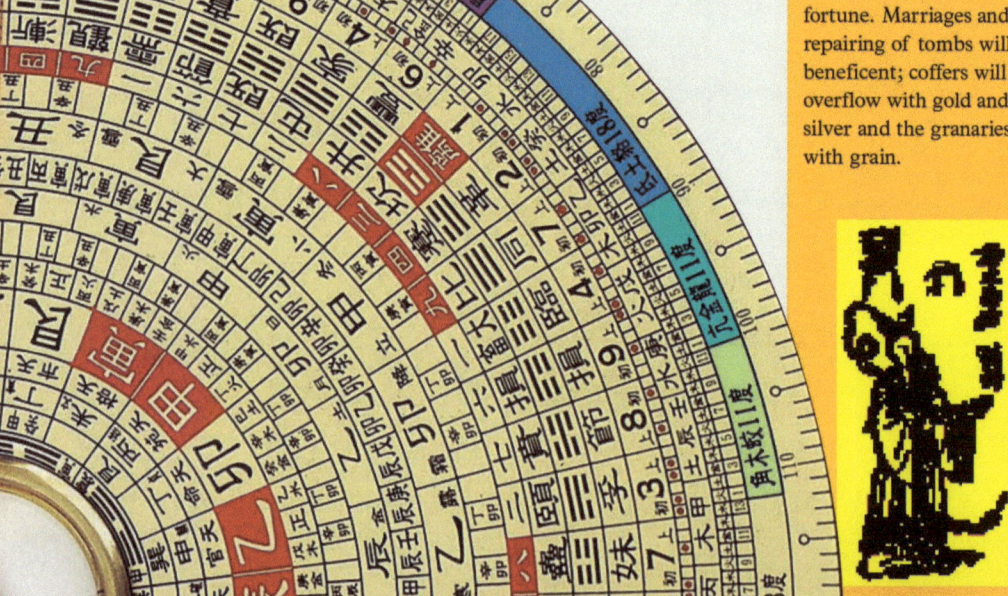

**The Basket (*Chi*), auspicious.**

To build today gives an assurance of power, and the beginning of any enterprise will assure the family the greatest good fortune. Marriages and the repairing of tombs will be beneficent; coffers will overflow with gold and silver and the granaries with grain.

**The Tail (*Wei*), auspicious.**

To build today is to be assured of blessings and a numerous progeny. To undertake any business matter or to flood a paddy field will assure prosperity to your descendants. Funerals and marriages will lead to the ennoblement of the family and the obtaining of posts in the capital.

interesting reflections of the time. As you can see, most of these predictions are centred around family relationships, burials and the chance of success in the official examinations of imperial China, which was the ordinary people's one and only chance of wealth and power. Many predictions are also made about all kinds of ceremonial and ritual events, as well as the beginning of any activity, especially the construction of a house, mentioned repeatedly in these predictions and a typical feng shui concern.

The following are the constellations on the Eastern Quarter of the compass attributed to the green dragon. Each of them is inscribed on the *lo p'an*, or feng shui compass, with the number of degrees of the celestial circle it occupies. It has been suggested that each *hsiu* corresponds to part of the dragon's anatomy. ◉

### The Heart (*Hsin*), inauspicious.

To build today will be most inauspicious and everything will lead to ruin sooner or later. Similarly burials and marriages will be seen to be disastrous and will assure three years of repeated calamities.

### The Chamber (*Fang*), auspicious.

To build today assures wealth and abundant prosperity. The Spirits of Happiness, of Longevity, of Honour, of Riches and of Glory hasten to meet you. If funerals are celebrated today, officials will be promoted by three ranks.

### The Root (*Ti*), inauspicious.

To build on this day will be inauspicious enough, and the celebration of marriages will bring endless calamities. Journeys by boat will be shipwrecked. Funerals will cause the impoverishment of descendants.

### The Neck (*K'ang*), inauspicious.

Do not build on this day; let the eldest not take the succession; let nothing be undertaken for in the ten following days a disaster will occur. Funerals and marriages undertaken on this day may cause untimely death and will risk leaving widows in the house.

### The Horn (*Ch'io*), auspicious.

To whomsoever builds on this day, this constellation will bring glory and prosperity, and men of letters will be able to approach near to the throne of the Emperor. Marriages on this day will result in numerous posterity. But to repair a tomb or go to a funeral on this day may provoke a new grief.

# Chinese Almanac

IN THE PREVIOUS ISSUE WE LOOKED AT THE 28 LUNAR MANSIONS, OR *HSIU*. HERE WE EXAMINE THE 24 STELLAR POSITIONS (*HSING TSUO*) WHICH ALSO INFLUENCE OUR DESTINY, ACCORDING TO THE CHINESE ALMANAC.

At the beginning and end of the Chinese Almanac are charts showing the positions of various stars. Sometimes these are explained as the positions occupied by spirits 'on duty' who influence that particular direction for different lengths of time. The *Imperial Encyclopaedia*, which included many chapters on astrology and feng shui, lists more than 800 different stars or spirits which might appear in the charts. Only twenty-four of them, however, appear on a chart for a particular time. Some star-gods, for example, might appear only every twelve years, in which case they would take the place of another star which might normally have occupied that position. The second of the stars listed here, the Tzu Wei, or God of the Purple Crepe Myrtle, is the ruler of the Great Bear constellation, and gives its name to a special branch of Chinese Astrology. Some of the star-names here are names of single stars, while others are actually constellations. An example is the thirteenth, Wen Chang, which would be regarded by Chinese astronomers as a group of six stars close to the Great Bear.

1. **T'ien-fu star:**
   **Description: Tien K'uang, Insanity**
   Originally it represents the wealth of Heaven. If your destiny is tied to this star, then you will be wealthy. During some years you might have minor misfortunes, but you will be able to overcome them. With hard work there will be prosperity. To enjoy future success you need cultivation. When you encounter the auspicious star you will be able to run your life smoothly and wealth will be coming from Heaven.

2. **Tzu-wei star:**
   **Description: K'o She, Mouth and tongue**
   This star is originally for the emperors. You will step into success.
   Although the limitations on your luck might be hard, they will end. When you help others to fulfill themselves, you will reach a higher moral standard. In bad years you should support one another, to make a living and establish youselves. You need to be strong-willed, and your happiness lies in your dependence on yourselves.

3. **Lung-teh star:**
   **Description: An Lu, Peace and happiness**
   This star is the dragon god. When you encounter this star you will have happiness, although it will still require your own effort. Wealth and offspring come naturally, and it is well respected by others. This star brings you career; you will not have to be frustrated by poverty.

4. **Chiang-hsing star:**
   **Description: T'ien Ch'ai, Land and dwelling**
   This is an auspicious star. Your wishes for wealth will become true. There will be harvests following the rain. If encountered at the same time with an inauspicious star, the Chiang-hsing star can decrease your misfortune.

5. **Chian-feng star:**
   **Description: K'u Ch'i, Weeping and wailing**
   When this star is prominent, you should be cautious about conflicts and arguements with people. Caution is the best policy, because the worst conflict could lead to a prison sentence. There is hardship but generally you can enjoy peace. In your middle age your career luck will be like spring thunder, and fame and reputation follows.

6. **Hua-kai star:**
   **Description: Ku Kua, Orphan**
   Wealth and career prospects can be uncertain. You need patience and peserverence to get through hardships. Your children can achieve academic success and the female members of the family will be good housekeepers.

7. **Fei-lian star:**
   **Description: Rung Fu, Glory and prosperity**
   This star is a god of wind, which could bring illness. The illness could be long-term if encountered at the same time with other inauspicious stars. But if encountered with auspicious stars, the harm will be lessened.

8. **Chian-cheh star:**
   **Description: K'u Chue, Sorrowful parting**
   This is a star of romance. You could also have help from the wealth of your wife. For men, this star could mean promiscuity, whereas for women it could mean curiosity in new relationships.

9. **Kuo-yin star:**
   **Description: Chang Yin, Debauchery**
   This star is originally the star of the emperors. It symbolises power and authority. When encountering this star, there could be powerful officials in the family.

10. **Mi-yue star:**
    **Description: Chin Yin, Relatives in marriage**
    When encountering this star, there could be difficulties in pursuing career and wealth. If you are engaged in trade, you might have minor problems. If you could adapt yourself in time of crisis, problems will soon be dissolved.

11. **Wang-shen star:**
    **Description: Huan Lo, Joyous pleasure**
    This is the inauspicious star of disasters. You can encounter some real hardship. You need to try and dissolve problems without delay. Then you might be able to accumulate wealth gradually.

12. **Tien-teh star:**
    **Description: Pai Chue, Disruption**
    This is a star of mentors. When encountering this star, all bad luck will dissolve and it's good time to establish your career.

**13. Wen-chang star:**
   **Description: Wang Ts'ai, Prosperity and wealth**
Wen-chang is a god of righteousness and intelligence. When encountering this star, you can enjoy academic success at an early age. For women born in the position of Wen-chang, she will certainly have special talents.

**14. Yu-tang star:**
   **Description: Fu teh, Happiness and virtue**
This is a star of mentors and academic career success. When the fish turns into a dragon, fame and reputation follow.

**15. Lu-hsun star:**
   **Description: Chi Eh, Sickness and distress**
This is a star of wealth. When the road is blocked, you need to be patient. When a horse comes to a bamboo bridge, it has to back down. Be cautious. The master of a small kingdom is not better than a subject in a powerful kingdom.

**16. Tien-yi star:**
   **Description: Chin Ts'ai, Entering wealth**
This is a star of mentors. You are destined to succeed in pursuing career and wealth. You will be particularly successful in trade and commerce.

**17. Tien-kou star:**
   **Description: Chang Ping, Lengthy illness**
It is a star of a dog god, and it's destined to be a slave. When encountering this star, you should do good deeds.

**18. Yue-teh star:**
   **Description: Ssu Chao, Joyous proclamation**
This is an auspicious star of mentors. You are strong-willed when in poverty. Your diligence and hard work will benefit you in the long term. With the help of the Mentor, you'll enjoy a good marriage and prosperous career.

**19. Sang-men star:**
   **Description: Kuan Wang, Official of prosperity**
This is an inauspicious star. You need to be cautious when encountering bad luck. Do not go near funerals. Be cautious of what you say. Do good deeds to cultivate your morals, then you will be able to dissolve this misfortune.

**20. Kuan-fu star:**
   **Description: Kuan Kuei, Official of Honours**
This is the star of outer connections. You need to be cautious in what you do. Calm your spirit to retain your interests. Then you can get through problems.

**21. Ku-shen star:**
   **Description: P'o Ts'ai, Breaker of wealth**
This is a lonely star. There is uncertainty to your future. Family relations on all sides might see you with contempt. Friends don't stay. You need to be sincere in seeking help from above. Pain will pass and fortune will come.

**22. Hsuan-wu star:**
   **Description: Fa Chan, Developing**
This is an auspicious star, but you still have to be cautious. Be cautious particularly of burglary and robbery. Also try to avoid arguements with others. Pray to god and the White Tiger. Kuan-yin will dissolve your misfortune.

**23. Kuan-tsuo star:**
   **Description: Yu Fu, Granting happiness**
This is originally a star of officialdom. Problems might arise from lack of determination. The old saints often said that you should clean away the snow in front of your own door and never get involved with conflicts between others. With good morals, official position can come even from an ordinary family.

**24. Hsue-ren star:**
   **Description: Fa Chang, Execution ground**
This is an inauspicious star. You need to be cautious when encountering it. There are obstacles to the development of your career. Be strong and do not be frustrated by poverty.

■ *Thanks to Derek Walters for his advice on the 24 stellar positions.*

1. T'ien-fu star   2. Tzu-wei star   13. Wen-chang star   22. Hsuan-wu star

# ChineseAlmanac 24

**THE WHITE TIGER IS A VERY DESTRUCTIVE FORCE AND SHOULD ALWAYS BE BALANCED**

The White Tiger in feng shui is a very yin symbol in contrast to the yang Green Dragon. The White Tiger has long symbolised negativity, and a home or office or company name where the yin White Tiger overwhelms the Green Dragon is thought to have very bad feng shui. In the pages from the Tung Shu or Almanac, the White Tiger is literally seen as the cause disaster and disease.

1. "When the auspicious star Yi-ma visits, he becomes very involved with a beautiful woman. Her beauty is as clear as jade, although his encounter with her would mean the loss of (his) fortunes". There are many Chinese and Japanese stories of men be seduced by female fox spirits, and the pointer to the woman's food clearly indicates that she is a fox spirit disguised as a woman.

2. "When a white tiger (or leopard) enters your fate, disasters will come. There will be conflicts and confrontations. Either a car accident, blood shed, or loss of fortune as a result of a legal case. If you are female, there might be heart problems".

This picture shows the effect of the White Tiger star "entering" the fate, or becoming part of the destiny of the reclining man. A tiger and demon face stare out from his bedside.

3. "You will have grave problems if you encounter the star Sui Chuen. You will feel dizzy and your limbs will be sore. When encountering it, women feel anxious. It suggests there may be prison sentence or a funeral". The White Tiger (or literally leopard) is here drawn like a real creature, but this image refers to its very real effect on your destiny.

4. When you encounter the god of Lo Hou (literally net/web Monkey), illness comes in conjunction with the White Tiger star. Your limbs will be sore and your heart will be weak and Inauspicious forces come to surround you. The combination of two ill omened stars look fairly conclusive. Even the two bamboo stalks outside the window signify death.

Of course in all there pictures, an extreme outcome is portrayed, but the message is that fluctuations in our luck come from precisely measurable configurations, and are not random. The references to stars by the way are not either astrononomical or astrological.

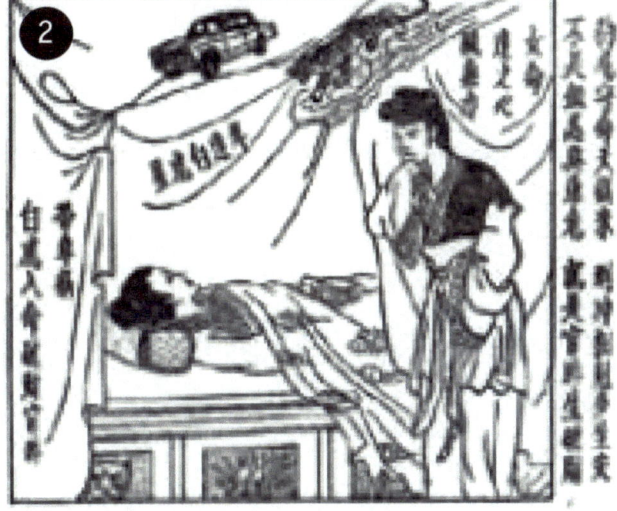

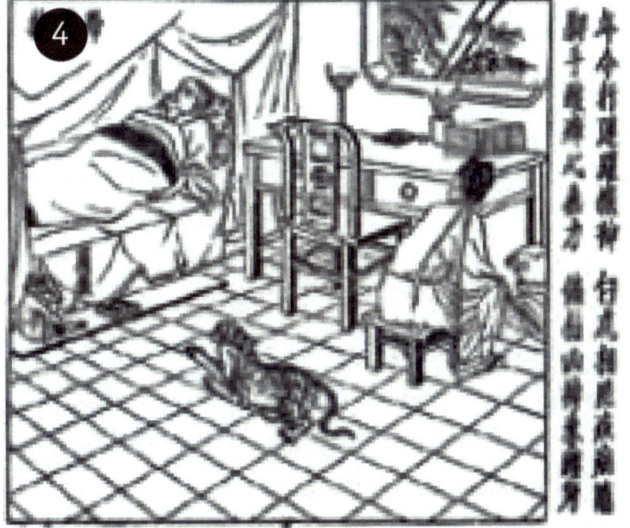

# ChineseAlmanac 25

THE TWELVE ZODIAC SIGNS ARE NEVER AN OUTDATED SUBJECT FOR ALMANAC READERS. THEY ARE CENTRAL TO CHINESE ASTROLOGY AND PROVIDE BASIC GUIDELINES TO PERSONALITY.

As most of you know, your Animal Sign comes from your birth year (see pages 84-85 to calculate which animal corresponds to your year of birth). The number 12 comes from the fact that the lunar calendar divides time into 60-year cycles made up of 12 years, multiplied by the Five Elements. The twelve years correspond to the Twelve Earthly Branches or Animal Signs.

The sequence of the twelve animals originate from the legend that these animals went to bid farewell to the Buddha, who then named each year after them sequentially to commemorate their loyalty.

The following pages from the Chinese Almanac show the compatibility of Signs with each other in relationships. These zodiac Animal Signs are divided into four groups of three, as shown in the diagram above. Each colour represents three Animal Signs compatible with each other, such as the blue triangle representing compatibility between the Snake, the Ox and the Rooster, or the yellow triangle representing compatibility between the Dragon, the Rat and the Monkey. The animals situated directly opposite each other are incompatible. For instance, the Horse is incompatible with the Rat, and the Rooster is incompatible with the Rabbit. The Rat and the Ox are particularly compatible. So are the Tiger and the Boar, the Rabbit and the Dog, the Snake and the Monkey, the Horse and the Goat (or Sheep). The Rat and the Horse are particularly incompatible. So are the Ox and the Goat (or Sheep), the Tiger and the Monkey, the Rabbit and the Rooster, the Dragon and the Dog, the Snake and the Boar. In the Almanac these compatibilities are illustrated by lovely drawings, four of which are reproduced here.

## COMPATIBILITY:

1. The Horse and the Goat (or Sheep) are compatible. They are the unity of *yin* and *yang*. It is by nature that they get along; their harmony lasts till old age. Their joy brings them excellent offspring. Fame and wealth visit their doorway.

2. The Monkey and the Snake are compatible. As a couple, their love is as strong as the (union of) stone and metal. In their early life they might be poor, but they prosper in their middle age. As husband and wife, the Monkey and the Snake are like the mandarin ducks playing in a lotus pond. Their love will last till old age; they will enjoy fortunes for three generations.

# FENG SHUI FOR MODERN LIVING

This page from the Almanac shows the unity of dragon and phoenix symbolising the highest level of compatibility, the reunion of *yin* and *yang*. The character at the top of the picture is a stylised version of the Double Happiness character. The text at the bottom is a speech made by the 'honorable guest' (usually a relative or close friend), introducing the bride and bridegroom to the wedding guests. It includes a description of their personalities and brief wedding greetings. The text at the bottom is a speech made by the chairperson of the ceremony, usually the parent of the bridegroom. Reference in these speeches will usually be made to the compatibility of the couple's Animal Signs.

## INCOMPATIBILITY:

3. The Monkey and the Tiger are incompatible. They might be fearful of change; their worst doubt is female infidelity. There is no concentration on the attainment of success. There is no will for studying; opportunities for careers might be abandoned. There is constant desire to part. Affairs are difficult to avoid.

4. The Rooster and the Rabbit are incompatible. They have different views and argue constantly. Things go against their wishes in earning a living. Tensions and disagreements grow. If they intend to resolve their conflicts, they need to choose the right time and the right day.

# ChineseAlmanac 26

THE TWELVE PALACES SHOULD NOT BE CONFUSED WITH THE TWELVE HOUSES. THE PALACES WERE ORIGINALLY THE NAMES OF THE TWELVE PHASES THROUGH WHICH THE FIVE ELEMENTS PASSED DURING THE MONTHS OF THE YEAR.

These Elements are passed in the same order as the Production order. Of the twelve, ten of them are probably of astrological origin, to which are added conception at the beginning and burial at the end. They form a full life cycle.

In the Almanac each of the Palaces is drawn as if it was a garden. The name of the palace is inscribed in Chinese in the top right hand corner. In the garden itself there are various hints as to the real secret nature of the Palace being illustrated. Some of these hints refer to feng shui. In this issue we choose three Palaces which mark major life stages. The first, Chang Sheng is birth but it also indicates growth or even the Palace which determines the total length of life. The second, Kuan Tai is literally the coming of age or reaching manhood. The third is Ssu Kung which is the Palace of Death. These three Palaces therefore describe three of the main life events. Look carefully at each illustration and you will see that they all feature a formal garden containing plants with ballustrades marking off the garden areas. In the garden of the first two Palaces are a variety of roses and intricately worn feng shui rocks. Both these are entered through a moon gate which regulates the flow of *ch'i*. In the sky in the first and third picture are supernatural beings, and in amongst the rose bushes of the second is a hidden dragon.

## 12 Palaces

| | |
|---|---|
| shou ch'i | to receive breath (conception) |
| t'ai kung | womb |
| yang kung | nourishment |
| chang sheng | growth, or to be born (sometimes length of life) |
| mu yu | to be cleansed |
| kuan tai | to come of age (literally to assume official cap and girdle) |
| lin kuan | to attain officialdom |
| ti wang | prosperity |
| shuai kung | to decay (become weak) |
| ping kung | to become sick |
| ssu kung | death |
| tsang kung | to be buried, burial |

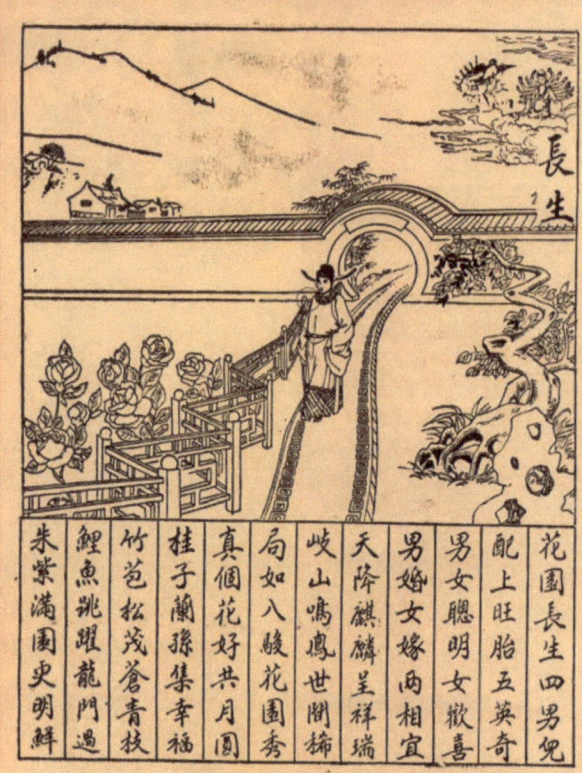

**Fourth Palace: Chang Sheng (Birth)**

"The descending of a Quirin to Earth brings great fortune. Life prospers like the growth of a garden. There is natural balance in the union of a man and a woman…bringing happiness and prosperity like the growth of orchid and pine trees…Fish jumping over the Dragon gate…brightness reflected in a garden filled with red and purple colours."

"Fish jumping over the Dragon gate" symbolises career/academic success. The fish which suceeds turns into a dragon. Of all the eight aspirations, such as a happy marriage or career success, all contribute eventually to longevity. In the sky is a many armed god and a bird. The garden entrance is a moongate and the herd zig-zags, so as not to create a "poison arrow."

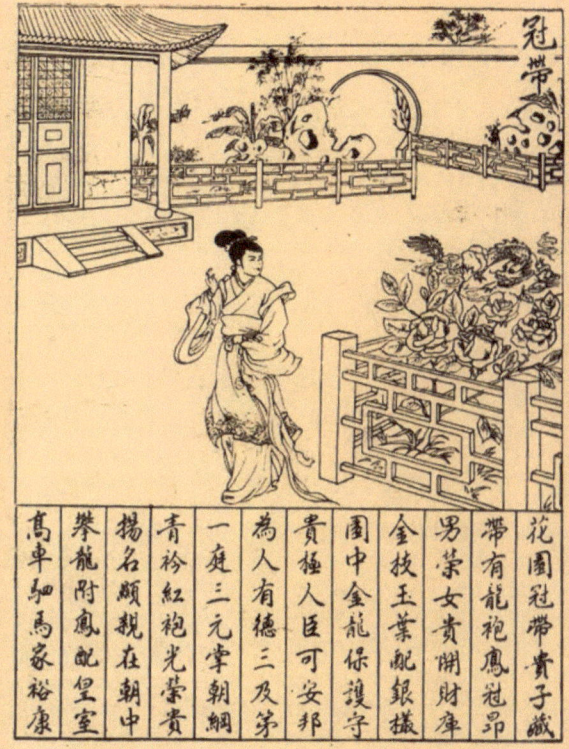

**Sixth Palace: Kuan Tai (Coming of age)**

"A precious son wears the Dragon robe...fame and fortunes flow in. Golden branches, jade leaves and silver bushes...all surrounding the guardian Metal Dragon in the garden. His virtues set the rules, and his name brings glory to the family."

Kuan Tai also means fame because it implies the crown and belt of honour or office. Look carefully in the flowers and you will see the hidden metal dragon.

**Eleventh Palace: Ssu Kung (Death)**

"Pine, bamboo and plum blossoms are the three friends of winter time in the garden. If married to a man of auspicious *pa tzu*, you naturally have the offspring of the Dragon and Phoenix. If married to the wrong man, you would have different dreams in the same bed. And you might not have children. There might be wealth, but it would be divided up."

Winter time refers to death. The *pa tzu* is the horoscope af eight characters or Four Pillars.

# Chinese Almanac 27

IN THIS ISSUE WE CONTINUE WITH THREE MORE OF THE TWELVE PALACES.

The Twelve Palaces show the twelve stages of life from conception to death. These texts, like many in the Almanac, are written in a poetic fashion and so some of their meaning can be very ambiguous. Here we have tried to give a literal interpretation.

### Second Palace T'ai Kung (Palace of the Womb):

After the first Palace of conception comes the second Palace of the Womb.

"Palace T'ai Kung in the garden refers to femininity. There are seven stars surrounding the moon. The inauspicious god is holding an axe in his hand. You should be respectful to your parents; your piety may touch the heart of the god. The Heavenly Emperor may bestow favours and give you a son, who may achieve promotion, offcialdom and the family may prosper for up to five generations. Inside the walls there are more flowers than fruits. Outside the walls there are fragrant almonds, pears and peaches. If your ancestors have accumulated virtues, the girl child may become an empress or a concubine. If you act in a virtuous way, you may change your destiny".

The axe holding god may threaten the unborn child. Piety is supposed to be your protection against this god. You might find "filial piety" an alien concept, but it is part of traditional Chinese culture, and something consistently mentioned in the Almanac. The importance attached by the Chinese to having a son and the idea of continuing the family line are clearly demonstrated in this text and literally in the title of the palace itself, the Womb Palace. Becoming an official was the route to prosperity and moving up the social scale. The peach symbolises female fertility. If you have a girl child, under these circumstances, even she may become famous.

### Third Palace Yang Kung (Nourishment or Nurture):

This Palace refers to the nourishment of the child.

"The Palace Yang Kung in the garden refers to only having a few sons. The spider threads its web in the garden. Whether a son or a daughter, the wedding would be a joyous one. Although it is always a joy to have a daughter-in-law, you shed tears when your own daughter gets married. The ideal would be to acquire a son-in-law, so that you have both your daughter and a son in the family. Who knows what could last through a storm? When it comes to accumulating virtues and cultivating merits, the men excel."

The spider's web is a traditional Chinese symbol. Interestingly the feng shui compass or *lo p'an* also means a net or a web, which is a suggestive connection. The feng shui stones in the garden are in this Palace particularly phallic.

### Fifth Palace Mu Yu (Cleansing):

This Palace comes after the Chang Sheng Palace (run in Issue 28). Chang Sheng is growth and in some sense the fixing of the length of life. Mu Yu refers to personal cultivation both spiritually and intellectually.

"When Mu Yu is in the garden, flowers bloom and fade. Mu Yu was originally a Tao Hua (which are peach blossoms, referring to romance and affairs) constellation. Tao Hua grows handsomely in the garden. With Heaven as the guardian it should be a happy couple, and their son and daughter would grow up well. When it rains in the old garden, the grass gives a fragrant smell. You may have a son-in-law like a dragon in your old age. The pines trees are green and crisp; the clouds cover the moon. An old oyster breeds a pearl; the sun rises in the east."

Here the Palace has a deep pond which relates to the idea of ritual bathing. The second half of the commentary contains general sayings. The "old oyster breeds a pearl" refers to the possibility of even an old person producing a child.

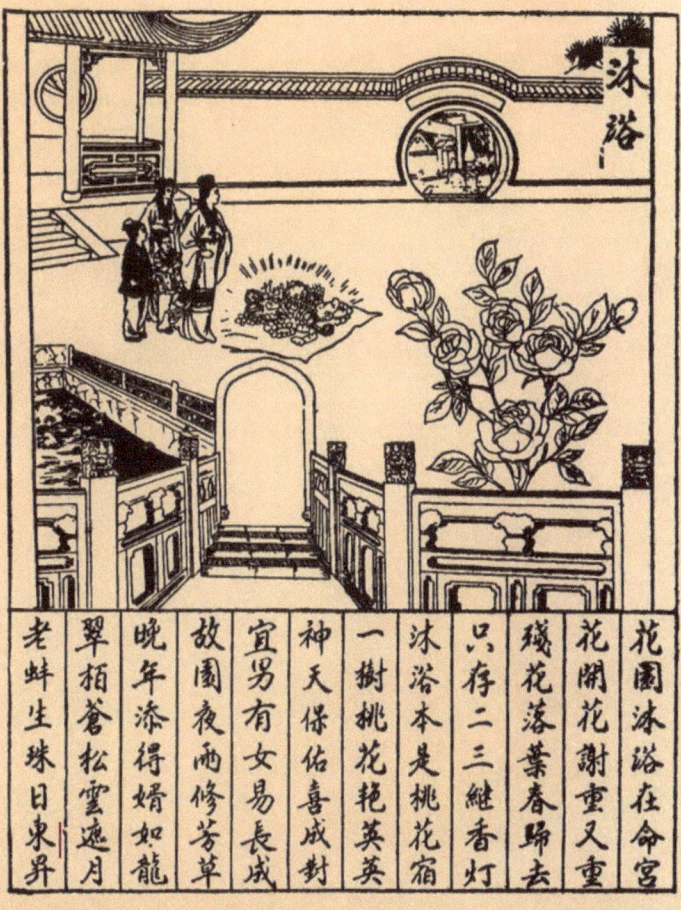

# ChineseAlmanac 28

THE TWELVE PALACES SHOULD NOT BE CONFUSED WITH THE TWELVE HOUSES. THE PALACES WERE ORIGINALLY THE NAMES OF THE TWELVE PHASES THROUGH WHICH THE FIVE ELEMENTS PASSED DURING THE MONTHS OF THE YEAR.

These Elements are passed in the same order as the Production order. Of the twelve, ten of them are probably of astrological origin, to which are added conception at the beginning and burial at the end. They form a full life cycle.

In the Almanac each of the Palaces is drawn as if it was a garden. The name of the palace is inscribed in Chinese in the top right hand corner. In the garden itself there are various hints as to the real secret nature of the Palace being illustrated. Some of these hints refer to feng shui. In this issue we choose three Palaces which mark major life stages. The first, Chang Sheng is birth but it also indicates growth or even the Palace which determines the total length of life. The second, Kuan Tai is literally the coming of age or reaching manhood. The third is Ssu Kung which is the Palace of Death. These three Palaces therefore describe three of the main life events. Look carefully at each illustration and you will see that they all feature a formal garden containing plants with ballustrades marking off the garden areas. In the garden of the first two Palaces are a variety of roses and intricately worn feng shui rocks. Both these are entered through a moon gate which regulates the flow of *ch'i*. In the sky in the first and third picture are supernatural beings, and in amongst the rose bushes of the second is a hidden dragon.

## 12 Palaces

| | |
|---|---|
| shou ch'i | to receive breath (conception) |
| t'ai kung | womb |
| yang kung | nourishment |
| chang sheng | growth, or to be born (sometimes length of life) |
| mu yu | to be cleansed |
| kuan tai | to come of age (literally to assume official cap and girdle) |
| lin kuan | to attain officialdom |
| ti wang | prosperity |
| shuai kung | to decay (become weak) |
| ping kung | to become sick |
| ssu kung | death |
| tsang kung | to be buried, burial |

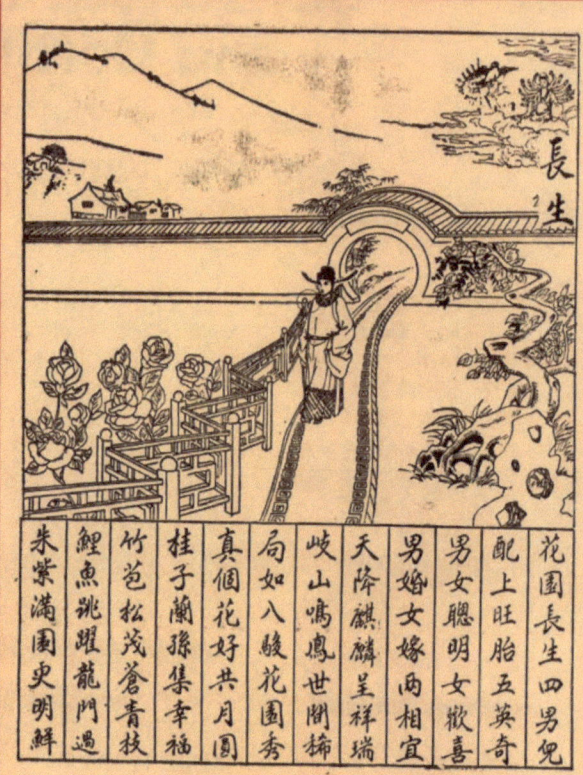

### Fourth Palace: Chang Sheng (Birth)

"The descending of a Quirin to Earth brings great fortune. Life prospers like the growth of a garden. There is natural balance in the union of a man and a woman...bringing happiness and prosperity like the growth of orchid and pine trees...Fish jumping over the Dragon gate...brightness reflected in a garden filled with red and purple colours."

"Fish jumping over the Dragon gate" symbolises career/academic success. The fish which suceeds turns into a dragon. Of all the eight aspirations, such as a happy marriage or career success, all contribute eventually to longevity. In the sky is a many armed god and a bird. The garden entrance is a moongate and the herd zig-zags, so as not to create a "poison arrow."

# FSML ALMANAC HANDBOOK

This version of the Chinese Almanac contains both solar and lunar calendars, with the moon determining the length of each lunar month and the sun governing the length of the year. The solar calendar is divided according to the 24-cycle period of a farmer's calendar, based upon weather changes and times of harvests. The overall divisions are called *Chieh/Ch'i*, each of which corresponds to 15 degrees of the sun's movement and is equal to about 15-16 days. The time character of the 24 divisions correlates with the space dimension on the *lo p'an* compass which is divided into 24 'Mountains' or directions. Thus, the use of the compass integrates the time and space into one single system (See Stephen Skinner, *The Living Earth Manual of Feng Shui*, 1982).

Among the 24 divisions, White Dew (*Pai Lu*) begins on 8 September, as shown on this almanac page. This section also gives the time of sunrise and sunset.

The Mid-Autumn Festival is marked in blue. You can see the date is 12 September (solar calendar) or 15th of the 8th month (lunar calendar).

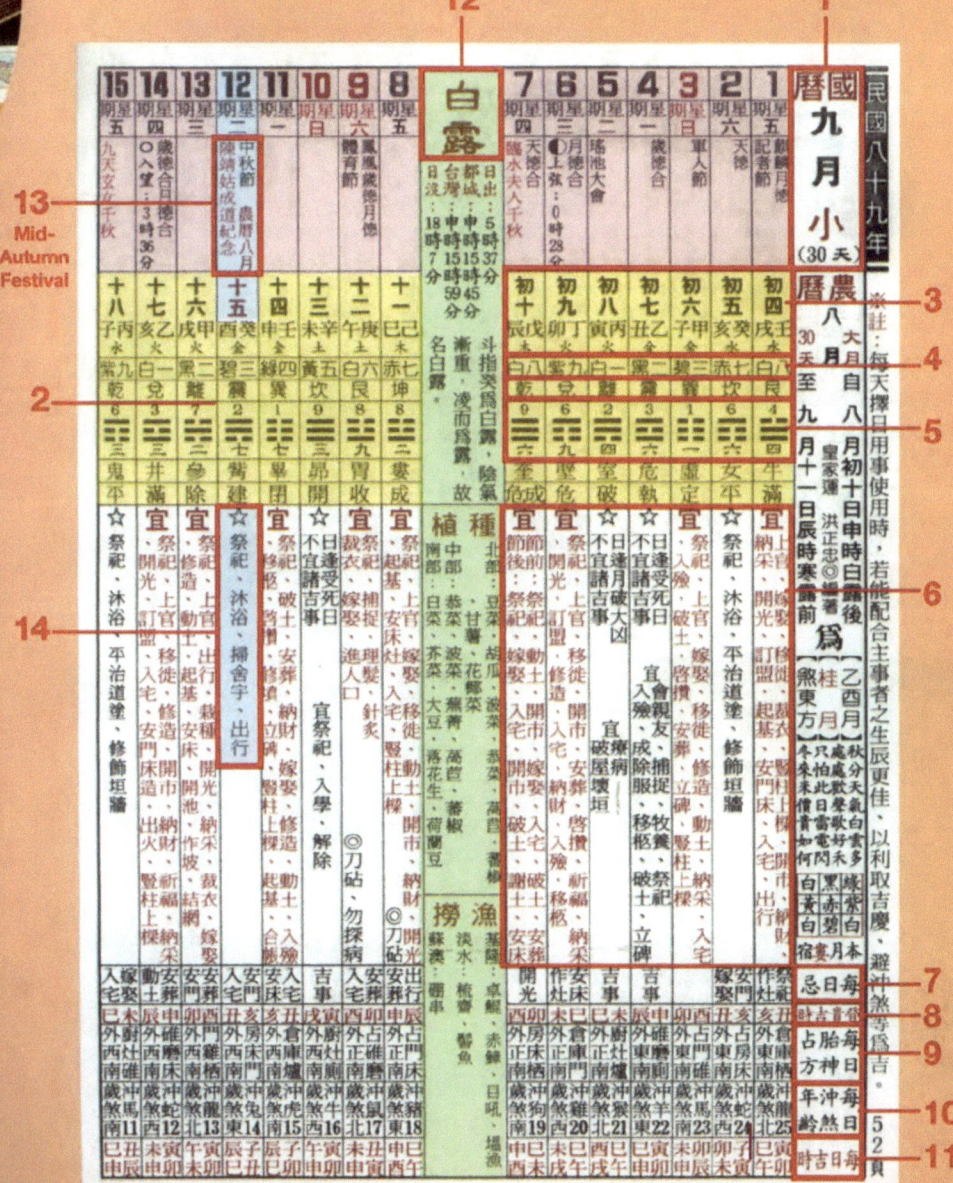

1. The Solar calendar is the top pink block, with the numbers indicating the days of the Western or solar calendar. This month is September, a 'small month', with 30 days.

2. Lunar calendar (marked in yellow), comes below the solar calendar with days marked in Chinese numbers. The bottom of the blue panel indicates 15th day (lunar calendar) of the 8th lunar month.

3. Dates, Branches and Stems, Elements of the day.

4. Nine stars

5. One of the Eight Trigrams for each day.

6. Auspicious activities for each day

7. Inauspicious activities for each day

8. Auspicious hours for prosperity

9. "Womb god" indication for each day

10. Inauspicious ages for each day

11. Auspicious hours for each day

12. White Dew, one of the 24 *ch'i*.

13. Mid-Autumn Festival

14. Auspicious activities on the day of the Mid-Autumn Festival are not surprisingly worship, bathing, cleaning and sweeping, travelling.

www.ingramcontent.com/pod-product-compliance
Lightning Source LLC
Chambersburg PA
CBHW042012150426
43195CB00003B/102